KAREN BROWN'S

French
Country Bed & Breakfasts

OTHER KAREN BROWN TITLES

Austrian Country Inns & Castles

California Country Inns & Itineraries

English Country Bed & Breakfasts

English, Welsh & Scottish Country Hotels & Itineraries

French Country Bed & Breakfasts

French Country Inns & Itineraries

German Country Inns & Itineraries

Irish Country Inns

Italian Country Bed & Breakfasts

Italian Country Inns & Itineraries

Portuguese Country Inns & Pousadas

Scandinavian Country Inns & Manors

Spanish Country Inns & Paradors

Swiss Country Inns & Chalets

KAREN BROWN'S

French Country Bed & Breakfasts

Written by

KIRSTEN PRICE and **CLARE BROWN**

Sketches by Barbara Tapp

Cover Art by Jann Pollard

Karen Brown's Country Inn Series

Editors: Karen Brown, Clare Brown, June Brown
Kirsten Price, Iris Sandilands
Technical support: William H. Brown III, Aide-de-camp: William H. Brown
Illustrations: Barbara Tapp, Cover painting: Jann Pollard
Maps: Cassell Design

This book is written in cooperation with:
Town and Country - Hillsdale Travel, San Mateo, CA 94401

Copyright© 1989 1992 by Karen Brown's Guides

Distributed by
The Globe Pequot Press, 138 West Main Street, Chester, CT 06412

Library of Congress Cataloging-in-Publication Data

Price, Kirsten, 1956
    Karen Brown's French country bed & breakfasts / written by Kirsten
Price and Clare Brown.
            p.   cm. -- (Karen Brown's country inn series)
    Includes index.
    ISBN 0-930328-03-5 : $13.95
    1. Bed and breakfast accommodations--France--Guide-books.
2. France--Description and travel--1975--Guide-books. I. Brown,
Karen. II. Brown, Clare. III. Title. IV. Title: French country
bed & breakfasts. V. Title: French country bed and breakfasts.
VI. Series.
TX907.5.F7P75 1992
647.944403--dc20
                                                      91-40775
                                                        CIP

Dedicated to

Bill

Who Had Forgotten

The Beauty of France

Contents

Introduction

Travellers with a sense of adventure can truly experience France, the French people and their culture by journeying beyond Paris and exploring the countryside. The way of life outside Paris, in "the provinces", as the French say, is a fascinating reflection of French history and culture: the impact of modern civilization is felt, but a pronounced respect for traditions and quality of life remains. Beyond Paris, the land is like a treasure chest filled with wonders of nature and civilization. There are royal forests still inhabited by stags and wild boars, graceful castles beside peaceful lakes, picturesque stone and half-timbered villages, colorful vineyards and farmlands, medieval walled cities and wild, salty coastlines all waiting to be discovered.

The bed and breakfast formula is for any traveller who wants to experience the "real" France, its people and culture. Single travellers will love the social aspect of bed and breakfast stays: there are ample opportunities to meet other friendly travellers, usually Europeans, as well as the hosts and their families. We have made many lasting contacts and friends through our research and travels. Families with children will enjoy the informality, convenience and reasonable rates of the "Chambres d'Hôtes" system.

Bed and breakfasts are called "Chambres d'Hôtes" (literally "guest bedrooms" in French) and are usually found in rural setting. This guide offers lodging selections in or near major tourist sites, as well as in unspoilt, less visited regions. Most hosts prefer that their bed and breakfast guests take the time to unwind by staying at least two nights. (Americans have a reputation for always being in a HURRY). Frequently stays of a week are discounted, but the advantages of longer stays in one place are far greater than just financial. It is great fun to become friends with the owners and other guests, to just "settle in" - no packing and unpacking every night. Strongly consider the possibility of choosing one place to stay and make it your hub, going off in a different direction each day to explore.

European hotels in a price range comparable to most bed and breakfasts tend to all be cut from the same cloth: sterile, sometimes even dingy and depressing. For the same price or less, bed and breakfast accommodation is personal, usually superior in cleanliness and comfort, and as varied as the landscape. Spend a night in a chateau dating from the Middle Ages whose stone walls evoke dreams of knights and their ladies, and the next night experience the sights and sounds of a simple farm surrounded by bucolic pasturelands. Careful reading of the descriptions in this guide will ensure that the homes you select are in line with the type of welcome and accommodation you prefer. Each home is, of course, unique, offering its own special charm, yet all share one wonderful common denominator: the welcoming feeling of being treated as a cherished guest in a friend's home.

There are 3,800 bed and breakfasts that are members of a French national organization named GÎTES DE FRANCE. We worked very closely with this organization which gave us tremendous cooperation in helping us select the very finest places to stay from an overwhelming list. We also visited and have included homes offering accommodation that are not part of Gîtes de France: the few bed and breakfasts that are independent of the Gîtes organization are featured in the descriptions with an asterisk by their name.

The Gîtes de France logo, as shown below, is usually painted in yellow and green and referenced on signs of most member bed and breakfasts.

Introduction

Bed and breakfasts that are members of Gîtes de France conform to certain standards of welcome and comfort that are governed by the organization. Gîtes de France has a national office located in Paris that offers additional information and a complimentary reservation service. Their office is located at 35, rue Godot de Mauroy, 75009 Paris, France, telephone: 1.47.42.20.92, fax: 1.47.42.73.11. (Precede all phone calls to France with the country code 33.) English speaking staff is usually available to answer questions and offer assistance. There is also a Loire Valley office for regional reservations: Gîtes de France - Indre et Loire, 38, rue Augustin Fresnel, B.P. 139, 37171 Chambray les Tours Cedex, France, telephone: 47.48.37.12, fax: 47.48.13.39. English is also spoken at the Loire Valley office and reservation assistance is free. The Dordogne region's Gîtes de France office prefers bed and breakfast reservations be made through their office and their address and phone number is: Gîtes de France, 16 rue Wilson, 24009 Périgeux, telephone 53.53.44.35, fax: 53.09.51.41.

We personally visited over 350 bed and breakfasts throughout France and, whether they were recommended as members of Gîtes de France or independent, we made our own personal selection based on their individual charm, ambiance and welcome. Each bed and breakfast described and recommended was inspected by us and was chosen by merit alone - none of the places to stay paid to be included in this guide.

ACCOMMODATION

Bed and breakfast accommodation, in most cases, means a bedroom rented in the home of a French family. Throughout this guide, the French term "chez" used before a family name translates as "at the home of" and is an accurate phrase when describing the type of accommodation and ambiance that one can expect. Lodging arrangements range from basic rooms sharing the family's living area and bathroom facilities to completely independent apartments, and include many degrees in between. Many of the accommodations listed herein offer a separate guest entry and private bath facilities.

Levels of comfort and luxury are as individual and varied as the people and homes you will be visiting, so look at the rates and read the descriptions carefully in order to ensure finding the desired type of accommodation. All of the bed and breakfasts listed in this guide are clean and tidy and, unless otherwise specified, have at least a basin area in the bedroom if there is no private bath. Sometimes in the least expensive bed and breakfasts toiletries are not provided, not even soap; so bring your own. (On the other hand, some of the more elaborate bed and breakfasts offer every nicety including shampoo and hair dryer.) Besides soap, two other items that are a good idea to pack are a face-flannel and a flashlight. The former is almost unheard of in France, and the latter can be helpful for a middle-of-the-night trip to the hallway WC.

Hosts cover the entire spectrum of French society, from titled counts and countesses to country farmers. All who are listed in this guide are hospitable and have a true desire to meet and interact with their guests. It takes a special kind of person to open his home to strangers, and the French who do so are usually genuinely warm and friendly. Bed and breakfast accommodation is actually a relatively new trend in France, only gaining popularity in the last five to ten years. By nature a reserved and private people, the French are beginning to let down some of the barriers that have prevented such contact with strangers in the past.

DRIVING AND DIRECTIONS

It is important to understand some basic directions in French when locating bed and breakfasts. Signs directing to Chambres d'Hôtes are often accompanied by either "1ère à droite" (first road on the right) or "1ère à gauche" (first road on the left). Chambres d'Hôtes signs can vary from region to region, but most have adopted the national green and yellow sign of the Gîtes de France as previously shown on page 2.

A Michelin map will label the roads with their proper number, but you will find when driving that signs usually indicate a direction instead of a road number. For example, instead of finding a sign for N909 north, you will see a sign pointing in the direction of Lyon, so you must figure out by referring to your map whether Lyon is north of where you want to go and if N909 leads there. The city that is signposted is often a major city quite a distance away. This may seem awkward at first, but is actually an easy system once you get your bearings.

Many bed and breakfast homes and farmhouses are located outside of whatever town or village they are listed under - the directions in this guide are especially helpful in getting you from the nearest village to your destination for the night.

However, if you become lost while looking for a bed and breakfast, you can always find the nearest post office or public phone box (usually in the central town square or in front of the post office) and call your hosts for directions - it is a good idea to keep a few francs handy for phone calls. In a pinch, bars and petrol stations will usually allow you to use their phones (they will charge you after the call).

MAPS: Purchase a regional Michelin map for every region where you will be travelling. Incredibly detailed, these indispensable maps list everything, even the smallest country lanes; as well as scenic viewpoints and historical monuments. Michelin maps can be purchased or special-ordered from travel-oriented book stores. Nothing can surpass the accuracy and detail of the Michelin maps, but, sadly, they lack an index; so, it is helpful to also purchase a paper-back atlas (such as Rand McNally or Recta Foldex) that has a detailed index. The directions in this guide to the bed and breakfasts are meant to supplement a detailed map, and in many cases are not sufficient on their own. When you are in France, maps can be purchased in a "librairie" (bookshop), a "tabac" (tobacconist), or at gas stations along the major auto routes.

LANGUAGE

Language is only sometimes a barrier, but a good idea is to take a travellers' French course before departure. Possessing even the most rudimentary knowledge and exposure to French will make your trip a thousand times more rewarding and enjoyable. One can always "get by": usually there is someone around who speaks at least a little English, and the French are accustomed to dealing with non-French-speaking travellers. It is helpful to carry paper and pencil to write down numbers for ease of comprehension, as well as a French phrase book and/or dictionary. If pronunciation seems to be a problem, you can then indicate the word or phrase in writing. If you are having difficulty, above all keep your sense of humor; becoming frustrated or angry only makes matters worse.

Levels of hosts' English are indicated according to the following guidelines:

NO English spoken - a few words at best.

VERY LITTLE English spoken - a little more than the most rudimentary, or perhaps their children speak schoolroom English. More is understood than spoken.

SOME or GOOD English spoken - basic communication is possible, but longer, involved conversations are not. Speak slowly and clearly and remember, they may understand more than they can articulate.

VERY GOOD English spoken - easy conversational English. More understood than able to express verbally.

FLUENT English spoken - can understand and communicate at about the same level; usually the person has lived in Britain or the United States.

MEALS

"BED AND BREAKFAST" usually provides a Continental-type breakfast, including a choice of coffee (black or with hot milk), tea or hot chocolate, bread (sometimes a croissant or wheat bread for variety), butter and jam served in the dining-room or kitchen, rarely in the bedroom. The evening before, hosts will customarily ask what time you want breakfast, and which beverage you prefer. Sometimes they will offer a choice of location such as outside in the garden, or indoors in the dining area or kitchen.

"TABLE D'HÔTE" means that the hosts serve an evening meal, usually sharing it with you, though certainly not always. This can be served at one long table with the hosts, at individual guest tables, or at several shared tables. Prices quoted are per person and sometimes include a table wine.

Expect at least three courses (an appetizer, a main course and dessert), often four or five (with salad and cheese being served as two separate courses between the entree and dessert). Contrary to popular belief, salad is not always served after the main course and thus may appear before or accompanying the main meal. Food is always delicious, and ranges from plain home cooking to more elaborate, refined cuisine. Even though it is indicated in the bed and breakfast description that *Table d' Hôte* is available, it is always only by reservation. So if you want to dine, be sure to tell your host when you book your room and check to see what time the meal will be served (be sure to call if you are running late). The French do not have large freezers stocked with frozen supplies nor microwaves to defrost a quick meal - food is usually selected and purchased with care the day it is to be prepared so it is difficult to produce an impromptu meal. If you are a late arrival and have not eaten, sometimes they will offer a plate of cold cuts, salad and bread; but do not expect this as it is not standard procedure.

"DEMI-PENSION" includes breakfast and dinner with prices quoted per person. This usually saves you money. Be sure to eat dinner, as hosts plan on it.

"PENSION COMPLET" includes breakfast, lunch and dinner with prices quoted per person. This formula is rarely an option since most travellers prefer to be on their own for lunches.

"FERME AUBERGE" is a family-style restaurant, also open to the public, on a working farm. These inns are actually controlled by the French government insofar as the products served must come mainly from the farm itself. Fare is usually simple and hearty, utilizing fresh meats and vegetables. The hosts do not usually sit down and share meals with their guests because they are too busy serving.

RATES

In each hotel listing, rates are usually given for single, double or triple accommodation, including tax, service and continental breakfast. Often rooms can accommodate up to four to six persons at additional charge. Cribs and extra beds are usually available for children. Prices usually go down if a stay is longer than three to five nights. "Gîtes" (small apartments) are often also available, and are ideal for families who prefer a bit of independence with cooking facilities. "Gîtes" rates do not include breakfast, are based on a week's stay, and are rarely available for shorter time periods. When budgeting, a rule of thumb to remember is that usually the farther out in the country and away from large towns or touristy regions, the more inexpensive accommodation will be. Beautifully furnished country homes and castles can be real bargains; but not if located in the highly popular Loire Valley.

RESERVATIONS/CANCELLATIONS

Especially during the busy summer months, reservations are vital, particularly for bed and breakfasts near the more touristy regions. Writing a letter is certainly the preferred method for booking accommodation, but allow plenty of time: it is advisable to write two months in advance so that you will have time to write to your second choice if your first choice is unavailable. Allow at least five days each way for air mail to and from Europe. A reservation letter in French with an English translation is supplied on page 12 at the end of the introduction. A few of the more sophisticated bed and breakfasts have installed fax machines, so if you have access to a fax, this is certainly the most efficient way to send a letter.

Telephone reservations are accepted by most bed and breakfast homes, but if you do not speak French and they do not speak English it will be frustrating and difficult to communicate your wants. However, for those bed and breakfasts that are members of the Gites de France organization, you can contact the Paris, Loire Valley or Dordogne offices (addresses and telephone information provided beginning on page 2) - English is spoken and they can assist you with reservations. Remember: to call or fax France, dial 011 (the international code) then 33 (the country code for France) and then the telephone number given in the description of the bed and breakfast.

Deposits are preferred if you are reserving several months ahead of your arrival date and should be paid in French francs. This is for your own protection against fluctuating exchange rates. Money orders in French francs can be purchased at the main branch of many large banks. Credit cards are rarely accepted at bed and breakfast homes. Payment should always be in French francs, not travellers' cheques.

The bed and breakfasts are not hotels, they are private homes, and there is not always someone always "at the front desk" to check you in. Therefore, it is a great courtesy to call the day you are expected to reconfirm your reservation and to advise approximately what time you expect to arrive. You can call from along the way from a public telephone (they are easy to use in France) or else call from where you stayed the previous night.

If it is necessary for you to cancel your reservation, PLEASE PHONE (or write far in advance) to alert the proprietor. Bed and Breakfasts often only have one or two rooms to rent, and are thus financially severely impacted if they hold a room for a "no-show". It is embarrassing to hear stories from gracious innkeepers who have stayed up until late at night, waiting to welcome the guest who never came.

TOURIST INFORMATION

"Syndicat d'Initiative" is the name for the tourist offices found in all towns and resorts in France (these offices are usually indicated by a sign with a large "I" - for information). These tourist offices are pleased to give advice on local events, timetables for local trains, buses and boats, and often have maps and brochures on the region's points of interest. They can also help with locating bed and breakfast and hotel accommodation.

In the United States, information can be obtained by writing or calling the French Government Tourist Offices located at 610 Fifth Street, New York, New York 10020-2452, or 9454 Wilshire Blvd., Beverly Hills, CA 90212, or 2305 Cedar Springs Road, Dallas, TX, or 645 N. Michigan Avenue, Chicago, IL. Information by phone can be obtained by calling 1-900-990-0040. Calls to this number will be charged to your phone bill at the rate of $.50 per minute.

Visas are no longer required for stays of 90 days or less. Information regarding student and longer-stay visas is available by calling the French Consulate at 212-606-3600.

SAMPLE RESERVATION REQUEST LETTER

Bed and Breakfast name and address
Monsieur/Madame:

Nous serons _____ personnes. Nous voudrions réserver pour _____ nuit(s),

We have (number) of persons in our party. We would like to reserve for (number) nights,

du _____ au _____ ,
from   (date of arrival)   to (date of departure),

_____ une chambre à deux lits,   _____ une chambre au grand lit
    a room(s) with twin beds   _____ *a room(s) with double bed(s)*

_____ une chambre avec un lit supplémentaire,
    room(s) with an extra bed

_____ avec toilette et baignoire ou douche privée.
    with private toilet and bathtub or shower.

Nous serons _____ personnes.
We have   (number)   of persons in our party.

Veuilliez confirmer la réservation en nous communicant le prix de la chambre et la somme d'arrhes que vous souhaitez. Dans l'attente de votre réponse, nous vous prions d'agréer, Messieurs, Mesdames, l'expression de nos sentiments distingués.

Please advise availability, rate of room and deposit needed. We will be waiting for your confirmation and send our kindest regards.

Your name and address

Key Map

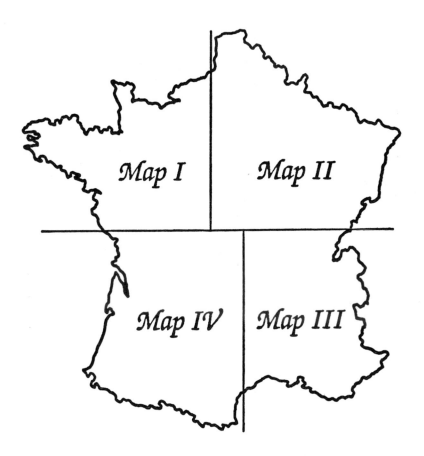

Map I

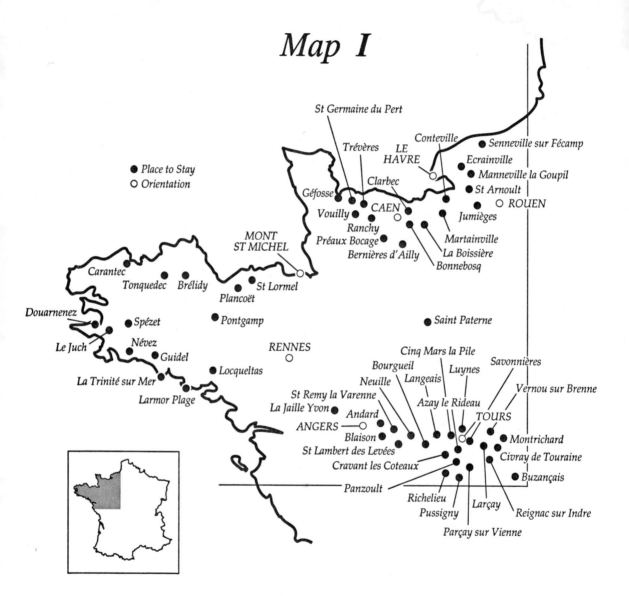

Place to Stay
Orientation

St Germaine du Pert
Trévères
Conteville
LE HAVRE
Senneville sur Fécamp
Ecrainville
Manneville la Goupil
Clarbec
St Arnoult
Géfosse
ROUEN
Vouilly
CAEN
Jumièges
Ranchy
Préaux Bocage
Martainville
Bernières d'Ailly
La Boissière
Bonnebosq

MONT ST MICHEL

Carantec
Tonquedec
Brélidy
St Lormel
Plancoët
Douarnenez
Spézet
Pontgamp
Saint Paterne
Le Juch
Névez
Guidel
RENNES
Cinq Mars la Pile
Savonnières
La Trinité sur Mer
Locqueltas
Bourgueil
Luynes
Vernou sur Brenne
Larmor Plage
Neuille
Langeais
St Remy la Varenne
Azay le Rideau
La Jaille Yvon
Andard
TOURS
ANGERS
Blaison
Montrichard
St Lambert des Levées
Civray de Touraine
Cravant les Coteaux
Buzançais
Panzoult
Richelieu
Larçay
Pussigny
Reignac sur Indre
Parçay sur Vienne

14

Map II

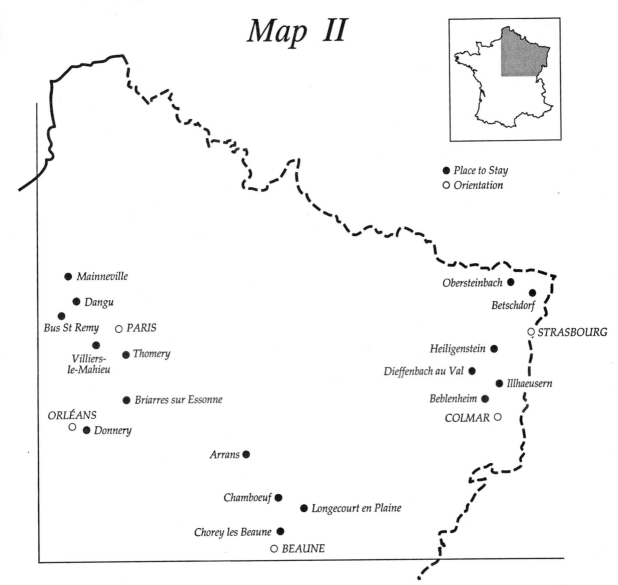

● Place to Stay
○ Orientation

● Mainneville

● Dangu

● Bus St Remy

○ PARIS

● Villiers-
le-Mahieu

● Thomery

● Briarres sur Essonne

ORLÉANS
○ ● Donnery

Arrans ●

Chamboeuf ●

● Longecourt en Plaine

Chorey les Beaune ●

○ BEAUNE

Obersteinbach ●

Betschdorf ●

○ STRASBOURG

Heiligenstein ●

Dieffenbach au Val ●

● Illhaeusern

Beblenheim ●

COLMAR ○

15

Map III

Charézier

Baudrières
Mancey
Géruge

Jaligny
Chatenay
Senozan
Bellevaux
Marcigny
MÂCON

● Place to Stay
○ Orientation

La Chapelle du Chatelard
Lhopital
Usinens
Les Villards sur Thônes

Villars les Dombes
ANNECY
Vesonne

Ordonnaz
LYON ○
Trevignin

Le Viviers du Lac
Montchavin

Chateaudouble
Bois Barbu

Étoile
Marsanne
Mirabel aux Baronies
Jansac
Freissinières

La Baume de Transit
Montmaur

Vaison la Romaine
Serres

Entrechaux
Crillon le Brave

St Pantaléon
Venasque

Le Caylar
Joucas

AVIGNON
Gordes
NICE

Pont du Gard
Rousillon

Boisseron
Éyragues
Lacoste
CANNES

St Georges D'Orques

Plaissan
Grans
Entrecasteaux

Aramon
Les Baux
St Martin-
de-Crau
MARSEILLE

16

Map IV

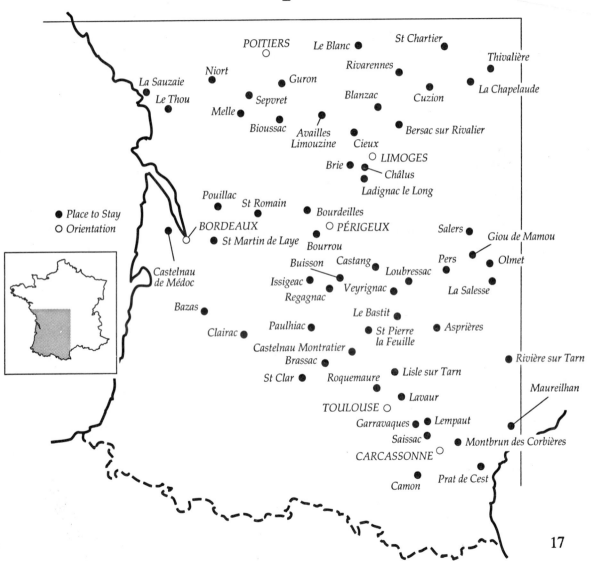

POITIERS ○   Le Blanc ●   St Chartier ●

Niort ●   Thivalière ●

Rivarennes ●   La Chapelaude

La Sauzaie ●   Guron ●   Blanzac ●   Cuzion ●

Le Thou ●   Sepvret ●

Melle ●   Bioussac ●   Bersac sur Rivalier ●

Availles
Limouzine ●   Cieux ●

Brie ●   LIMOGES ○

Pouillac ●   Châlus ●

St Romain   Ladignac le Long ●

Bourdeilles ●

● Place to Stay   PÉRIGEUX ○   Salers ●

○ Orientation   BORDEAUX ○   Giou de Mamou ●

St Martin de Laye ●   Bourrou   Pers ●   Olmet ●

Castelnau
de Médoc ●   Buisson ●   Castang ●   Loubressac ●

Issigeac ●   La Salesse

Bazas ●   Regagnac   Veyrignac ●

Clairac ●   Le Bastit ●

Paulhiac ●   St Pierre   Asprières ●
la Feuille ●

Castelnau Montratier ●   Rivière sur Tarn ●

Brassac ●

St Clar ●   Roquemaure ●   Lisle sur Tarn ●   Maureilhan

Lavaur ●

TOULOUSE ○

Garravaques ●   Lempaut ●

Saissac ●   Montbrun des Corbières ●

CARCASSONNE ○

Camon ●   Prat de Cest ●

17

Madame Guervilly's ivy-covered manor house dates from the 1700s and is filled with a collection of wonderful country antiques.   She is an antique dealer by trade and, fortunately for her guests, displays some splendid pieces in her historical home.   The breakfast room is particularly lovely, with old tile floors, high beamed ceiling and a massive stone fireplace, all complemented by period furniture. Madame enjoys entertaining friends and serving intimate Table d'Hôte dinners in this lovely room.   On warm mornings, guests are treated to breakfast on the garden terrace; a peaceful setting interrupted only by an occasional birdsong.   The charming guest rooms are found in a separate wing of the house where a restful night's slumber is assured after you are lulled to sleep by the rustling sound of the wind in the poplar trees. Picturesque surroundings, a gracious hostess and reasonable rates all combine to make Le Grand Talon a truly marvellous find. *Directions:* Andard is located 7 km east of Angers.   Leaving Angers, take N147 in the direction of Saumur.   After about 10 km, you will see a green and yellow Chambres d'Hôtes sign, 50 m later you'll see a large sign pointing to Sarrigne. Turn as if you were indeed going to Sarrigne, go through the stop sign and the driveway will be 20 meters later.

LE GRAND TALON
Hostess: Madame Annie Guervilly
Route National 147
49800 Trelaze, Andard, France
tel: 41.80.42.85
2 Rooms, both with private bath/share WC
Single: 180F, Double: 230F, Triple: 280F
Table d'Hôte: 100-200F per person
Open all year
Very little English spoken
Region: Loire Valley

Although close to Avignon, one almost seems in another world approaching through the barren, rock studded landscape to Le Rocher Pointu, a lovely old stone farmhouse softened by dark brown shutters and huge terra cotta pots brimming with flowers. It must have seemed an overwhelming task to make the house liveable when Annie and Andre Malek bought it a few years ago: there was not even running water. Now, not only is there running water, there is a beautiful swimming pool (if you are somewhat prudish, be forewarned that you might find most of the guests swimming au natural.) The interior has been renovated maintaining the natural appeal of the original old farmhouse: white walls, massive beamed ceilings, and country antiques add to the appealing ambiance. Upstairs are four bedrooms - my favorite is the Clair de Lune room with a handsome wooden, French Provençal headboard and a pretty view from the casement windows. There is a kithcen and barbeque area for guests' use. *Directions:* Aramon is located about 10 km southwest of Avignon. From Avignon, follow the D2 south along the west bank of the Rhône. Turn right, in the direction of Suze, when you come to D126. After 2.3 km you will come to the sign for Le Rocher Pointu. Turn left at the sign and follow the road to the Rocher Pointu.

LE ROCHER POINTU
Hosts: Annie & Andre Malek
Plan de Deve
30390 Aramon, France
tel: 66.57.41.87 fax: 90.85.58.51
4 Rooms, 4 with private WC/bath or shower
Single: 260-290F, Double: 280-310F, Triple: 400-445F
No Table d'Hôte
Open from March 15 to October 31
Good English spoken
Region: Provence

In a region where pretty Romanesque churches and medieval villages dot the rolling hills, very near the lovely and historic Fontenay Abbey, the Clergets offer modest and home-like accommodation in their pretty stone house. A charming front garden leads into Madame Clerget's friendly kitchen where her grandchildren often visit for a taste of her famous rhubarb pie. Guest bedrooms are located upstairs and are all unique, filled with an eclectic collection of knicknacks and antiques, old family photos, pictures and paintings. The house dates from 1807 and the rooms all have their own individual character, most with exposed beams and rafters.   Monsieur and Madame Clerget are a retired couple who extend a warm welcome to guests and are happy to aid in planning sightseeing excursions or even wild mushroom-hunting forays in the nearby forest. *Directions:* Arrans is located approximately 80 kilometers northwest of Dijon. Take autoroute A38 in the direction of Paris, exiting at Sombernon and continuing on D905 towards Vitteaux and Montbard. At the town of Montbard, turn right onto D5 towards Arrans. About 9 kilometers later, just before entering the village of Arrans, look for the Clergets' ivy-covered house on the left and marked with a Chambres d'Hôtes sign.

L'ENCLOS
Host: Mireille Clerget
Arrans, 21500 Montbard, France
tel: 80.92.16.12
4 Rooms, all w/ private WC, shower or bath
Single: 150F, Double: 200-250F, Triple: 300-350F
Table d'Hôte: 75-95F per person
Open March 1 through December 15
No English spoken
Region: Burgundy

Christiane and Serge Maurel's Ferme Auberge is built in a style typical of the more southern regions of France, with light stone walls and a warm tile roof. Accommodation consists of a suite in the main house and five rooms in a pavilion-style annex, each with French doors opening out to the swimming pool and lawn area. Rooms are clean and functional with cool tile floors and private bathrooms. The Maurels have created an idyllic setting, building their pool on a terrace overlooking a spectacular vista of faraway gorse- and oak-covered hills. Le Mas de Clamouze is well-known for its delicious meals served in generous portions. Days begin with a breakfast buffet of ham, yogurt, regional cheeses, fresh fruit, croissants, two kinds of bread, juice and a choice of coffee, tea or hot chocolate. In the evenings, Christiane's hearty, five-course meals featuring fresh farm produce are served in the spacious country dining room. *Directions:* Asprières is located approximately 16 kilometers southeast of Figeac. Take N140 towards Rodez as far as Bouillac, turning right onto D40 towards Villeneuve and Asprières. Go through the village of Asprières and follow Chambres d'Hôtes signs to the Maurels' farmhouse. The driveway is on the left-hand side of the road.

LE MAS DE CLAMOUZE
Hosts: Christiane and Serge Maurel
12700 Asprières, France
tel: 65.63.89.89
6 Rooms, all w/ private WC/bath or shower
Single: 157F, Double: 218F, Triple: 304F
Table d'Hôte: 78F per person
Open May 15 to September 15
Very little English spoken,
Some Italian & German spoken
Region: Lot

The small country village of Availles Limouzine is the peaceful setting for the 200-year-old home of Marie-Reine and Andre May. A shady front yard and sunny front terrace lead to the entrance of this quiet home where a warm welcome and comfortable quarters await. The Mays are still in the process of renovating some parts of their interesting house, but most of the public areas are freshly painted and home-like. Bedrooms are simply furnished and very clean, with artful touches adding life and charm. The entire family seems to have an artistic streak, and artwork by Madame's uncle, son and daughter is displayed throughout the house. The living room and dining room adjoin and are furnished in a pleasing mixture of country antiques and comfy seating accented by family photos. An adjoining terrace provides a pleasant spot for breakfast on sunny mornings. The modest Logis de la Mothe is recommended for travellers who are seeking quiet, comfortable accommodation in a village environment. *Directions:* Availles Limouzine is located approximately 56 kilometers southeast of Poitiers. Take D741 through Gençay, continuing to Pressac where you will turn left onto D34 to Availles Limouzine. Once in the village, go to the church at the top of the hill where the road splits: take the left fork. Look for the Mays' house on the right a few hundred feet later - the gatepost is marked with a Chambres d'Hôtes sign.

LOGIS DE LA MOTHE
Hosts: Marie-Reine and Andre May
86460 Availles Limouzine, France
tel: 49.48.51.70
4 Rooms, 2 with private bath/WC
Single: 125F, Double: 190, Triple: 250F
No Table d'Hôte
Open all year
No English spoken
Region: Limousin

Located just steps away from the well-known castle of Azay le Rideau, Madame Wilmann's refined home is a peaceful refuge for travellers. The aristocratic house dates from the 18th century and is entered by way of a sunny terrace and well-tended garden bursting with flowers. Inside, a lovely, spacious salon decorated in rose and blue hues sets an elegant, yet comfortable tone in decor and gracious welcome. Fragrant roses, freshly cut from Madame's garden, grace every room, while whimsical touches such as a hallway hat rack adorned with beribboned straw millinery reflect her artistic, imaginative style. Highly polished country antique furniture and tasteful colour schemes decorate the guest rooms, all of which have newly installed private bathrooms with showers. Bedrooms are not spacious, but Madame Wilmann happily puts her salon, terrace and garden at guests' disposal. *Directions:* Azay le Rideau is located approximately 22 kilometers southwest of Tours, and the route is well marked with easy-to-follow road signs. Once in the village of Azay le Rideau, follow signs which direct to the Chateau. Drive by the chateau gate, and turn into the second driveway on the right which is marked with a Chambres d'Hôtes sign.

LE CLOS PHILIPPA
Hostess: Madame Bernadette Wilmann
10, rue Pineau
37190 Azay le Rideau, France
tel: 47.45.26.49 or 47.48.37.13
4 Rooms, all with private shower/WC
Single: 250F, Double: 270-320F, Triple: 380F
No Table d'Hôte
Open all year
No English spoken
Region: Loire Valley

Nestled in the rolling hills and farmlands of the Lot region, the Chamberts' 150-year-old farmhouse has a regional red tile roof made remarkable by its twin pigeon towers at either end.   Guests have complete independence and privacy as the Chamberts live next door in a more recently constructed home.   Monsieur tends to his primary occupation of farming, while Madame capably handles all guest needs. A home-like, comfortable ambiance reigns, especially in the evenings when Madame serves her family-style Table d'Hôte dinners in front of the large open-hearthed fireplace. Beamed ceilings, hanging copper pots and rustic family antiques add warmth and charm to the homespun decor.   Bedrooms are equally charming; furnished in a mix of antiques and more contemporary pieces.   One particularly quaint room has a brass bed, exposed support beams and a pretty, round antique table adorned with an earthenware pot of dried flowers.   Located near the spectacular hillside village of Rocamadour, Domaine de Bel Air offers a quiet retreat into French farm life.   *Directions:* Le Bastit is located approximately 18 kilometers south of Rocamadour.   Take N140 towards Gramat and Cahors: at Gramat follow directions for Cahors and Le Bastit on D677.   At Le Bastit, look for a series of small, hand-made arrows directing you through the village and down a country lane to Domaine de Bel Air.

DOMAINE DE BEL AIR
Hosts: Francine Chambert
Le Bastit, 46500 Gramat, France
tel: 65.38.77.54
5 Rooms, 2 w/pvt WC/bath, others share
Single: 170F, Double: 200F, Triple: 260F
Table d'Hôte: 65F per person
Open all year
Very little English spoken
Region: Lot

Arlette Vachet's English-style country cottage is at the top of our list for romantic and atmospheric bed and breakfast accommodation. Arlette is a painter and former antique dealer who has filled her cosy, ivy-covered house with a potpourri of country antiques and used her artistic talents to decorate the interior to charming perfection. Her salon is a virtual treasure trove of paintings, old furniture and objets d'art, set off by low, beamed ceilings and an old stone hearth. A comfortable couch and a crackling fire are the perfect accompaniments to an evening's aperitif before sampling one of the region's many restaurants, renowned for their fine wines and gourmet cuisine. French doors open from the garden to the ground floor bedroom which is prettily decorated in tones of forest green and pink and has an adjoining rose-tiled bathroom. The upstairs bedroom is small and intimate, its walls and low, sloping ceiling covered by beautiful flowered wallpaper. Guests may use the pool for an additional 50F per day charge. *Directions:* Baudrières is located approximately 20 kilometers northeast of Tournus. Leave Tournus on N6 towards Sennecy le Grand and Chalon sur Saône. Just after passing through the town of Sennecy le Grand, turn right onto D18 in the direction of Gigny. Cross the river Saône and follow signs to the small village of Baudrières: Arlette Vachet's picturesque cottage is on the corner.

CHEZ VACHET
Hostess: Madame Arlette Vachet
Baudrières, 71370 St Germain du Plain, France
tel: 85.47.32.18
2 Rooms, both with private bath
Single: 200F, Double: 250F, Triple: 300F
No Table d'Hôte
Open all year
Good English spoken
Region: Burgundy

Ludovic and Eliane Cornillon have struck the perfect balance between rustic ambiance and luxurious comfort in their charming farmhouse found in the countryside of northern Provence.   The entire farm complex dates from 1769 and is rectangular in shape, forming a tranquil central garden sheltered by weathered stone walls.   A low doorway leads into the historic entry salon which has a large old hearth decorated with dried flower bouquets and interesting antique furniture including a petain, a piece somewhat like a large chest used for both storing flour and kneading bread dough.   The adjoining dining room, formerly the stables, still displays a stone feeding trough and little stairway to the attic where the hay was stored.   Eliane's fresh style of cuisine features regional herbs and is well complemented by Domaine de St Luc wines, as Ludovic is a talented winemaker. After dinner, a good night's rest is assured in charming bedrooms, all with spotless private baths.   *Directions:* La Baume de Transit is located about 24 kilometers north of Orange.   Take autoroute A7 and exit at Bollene, following directions for Suze la Rousse on D94.   Leave Suze la Rousse on D59 towards St Paul Trois Chateaux, but turn off almost immediately onto the small country road CD117 towards La Baume de Transit.   Look for signs for Domaine de St Luc.

DOMAINE DE ST LUC
Hosts: Ludovic and Eliane Cornillon
Le Gas du Rossignol, La Baume de Transit,
26130 St Paul-Trois Chateaux, France
tel: 75.98.11.51
5 Rooms, all with private bath/WC
Single: 200F, Double: 260F, Triple: 300F
Table d'Hôte: 125-130F per person
Open April 1 to October 30
Good English spoken by Eliane
Region: Northern Provence

As the road winds down the rocky barren incline from Les Baux, an oasis suddenly opens up where luxury hotels and handsome homes peek out from the shrubbery of verdant gardens. Here you will find La Burlande, the home of Jenny Fajardo de Livry: lawyer, mother, and talented "hotelier". At the moment she no longer practices law - her four children along with the day to day operation of La Burlande as a bed and breakfast keeps her more than occupied. The house is newly built and does not attempt to closely emulate the typical Provençal antique style. Instead, the ambiance is of a modern home with large picture windows and spacious bright, airy rooms. The furnishings, which are accented by oriental carpets on cool tiled floors, are sophisticated rather than "country-cute". There are only three guest rooms plus a suite comprising two guest rooms sharing a bathroom. This is an ideal set up for a family because it also has its own little terrace which opens out to a beautiful swimming pool and the impeccably tended, prize winning gardens. *Directions:* As you leave Les Baux on the D78F you will see Les Baux sign-posted on the left-hand side of the road.

LA BURLANDE
Host: Jenny Fajardo de Livry
Le Paradou
13520 Les Baux, France
tel: 90.54.32.32
3 Rooms with private bath/WC
1 2 bedroom suite sharing a bath
Single: 285-345F, Double 350-570F, Triple 520F+
Table d'Hôte: 125F per person
Open all year
Good English spoken
Region: Provence

The Chateau d'Arbieu is filled with family antiques, paintings, and objets d'art, yet also manages to convey a comfortable, lived-in feeling. Titled hosts Count and Countess de Chenerilles are a young, friendly and unpretentious couple who happily welcome guests to their historic family home. Delicious and carefully prepared Table d'Hôte dinners are enjoyed with the de Chenerilles in their pleasant dining room. Furnishings are a mix of contemporary and antique pieces accented by home-like touches such as large colour photos of their five children above the mantelpiece. The guest bedrooms which are found upstairs, affording lovely views over the countryside, contain beautiful antique furnishings and are decorated with tasteful, period-style wallpapers, fabrics and artwork. Fresh flower arrangements and in-room phones add thoughtful touches of luxury. Extensive grounds include a refreshing swimming pool and convenient poolhouse kitchenette for guests' use. *Directions:* Bazas is located 48 kilometers southeast of Bordeaux. Take autoroute A62 in the direction of Agen and Toulouse. Exit at Langdon and follow signs to Bazas via D932. From Bazas, take D655 towards Casteljoux and less than 1 kilometre outside town look for a Chambres d'Hôtes sign which marks the long driveway to the Chateau d'Arbieu.

CHATEAU D'ARBIEU
Hosts: Count and Countess de Chenerilles-Arbieu
33430 Bazas, France
tel: 56.25.11.18 fax: 56.25.90.52
4 Rooms, 1 Suite, all w/private bath or shower & WC
Single: 360-415F, Double: 385-440F
Table d'Hôte: 150F per person
Open all year (reservations required in winter)
Some English spoken
Region: Southwest

The picturesque Alsatian town of Beblenheim is the quaint setting for Stefan Klein's half-timbered antique shop, winebar, and bed and breakfast. Guests enter a flower-filled courtyard and then go down worn stone steps leading through an old archway to the atmospheric cellar bar where many convivial evenings are spent listening to music and sampling regional wines and beers. A light menu offers tasty gourmet fare such as quiche, salads and selections of regional cheese and sausage. Inviting guest rooms are located upstairs and are charmingly furnished with polished pine furniture, antique paintings, dried flower arrangements and cheerful, dainty, flowered bedspreads and pillowcases. Beamed ceilings and windows opening out onto flower-filled windowboxes complete the German country feeling. *Directions:* Beblenheim is located about 15 kilometers north of Colmar. Take N83 through the village of Ingersheim where you will turn right onto D10 and follow La Route des Vins (wine route) towards the town of Riquewihr. Turn off into the village of Beblenheim and follow the main street past a little fountain and the post office (PTT). Take the next right onto rue Jean Alace, followed by an immediate right onto rue des Raisins. The narrow street dead-ends, and Chez Klein is found at the end on the left.

CHEZ KLEIN
Host: Monsieur Stephan Klein
4, rue des Raisins
68980 Beblenheim, France
tel: 89.49.02.82
5 Rooms, all with private bath
Single: 200 Double: 245-270, Triple: 375F
Convivial, casual restaurant
Open all year
Good English spoken, also fluent German
Region: Alsace

High in the French Alps, life in the small, remote villages remains very much unchanged from generation to generation. A stay with the Pasquier family offers a chance to experience a real slice of mountain farm-life: no frills, but plenty of old-fashioned hospitality and simple comforts. Their traditional farmhouse is found nestled in a narrow valley flanked by green meadows and jagged peaks. The region is a paradise for hikers and skiers, all of whom the Pasquiers enjoy welcoming to their home and table. Madame's Table d'Hôte dinners feature substantial home-cooked fare typically including soup, a main course of meat and potatoes, a selection of cheeses, green salad and fresh fruit for dessert. Bedrooms are small but adequate with basic, yet pleasant decor; each with the convenience of its own tiny bathroom and WC. *Directions:* Bellevaux is located approximately 50 kilometers northeast of Geneva. Take D907 from Geneva for about 35 kilometers to the town of St Jeoire. Exit the national route and go into town, looking for a turnoff about halfway through town for Megevette. Continue through Megevette and look for a turnoff to the right just before the town of Bellevaux marked Chevrerie and Lac de Vallon. Pass the several chalets which make up the hamlet of Clusaz and look for a Chambres d'Hôtes sign marking a driveway on the right to the Pasquiers' farm.

CHEZ PASQUIER
Hosts: François and Geneviève Pasquier
La Clusaz, 74470 Bellevaux, France
tel: 50.73.71.92
5 Rooms, all with private bath/WC
Single: 90F, Double: 166F, Triple: 240F
Table d'Hôte: 65F per person
Open all year
No English spoken
Region: French Alps

This old stone farmhouse once belonged to the nearby chateau and is now an ideal stop for travellers seeking a familial, countryside bed and breakfast at a delightfully inexpensive price. Andre and Arlette Vermes and their three children welcome guests into their farmhouse with enthusiasm, always happy to assist guests by helping with sightseeing plans, loaning bicycles or even offering their playroom to children. The former stables comprise a separate wing for bed and breakfast guests which includes a large dining room/salon and three guest bedrooms. Downstairs, a rustic flavour still remains due to the collection of old farm implements displayed on the natural stone walls. Breakfasts and Table d'Hôte dinners are served here at a long pine table. The family-style meals feature regional dishes such as chicken in cream sauce and delicious apple tarts. Four bedrooms are found upstairs and one on the ground floor. Each is charmingly individualized with pretty details such as brass beds, pine armoires, pretty print wallpapers and matching bedspeads. Bathroom facilities are modern, well equipped and very clean. *Directions:* Bernières d'Ailly is located approximately 30 kilometers southeast of Caen, 10 kilometers northeast of Falaise on D511. In Bernières d'Ailly, follow the Chambres d'Hôtes signs which will direct you to the Vermes' farm.

FERME D'AILLY
Hosts: Andre and Arlette Vermes
14170 Bernières d'Ailly, France
tel: 31.90.73.58
5 Rooms, 3 w/private WC/bath or shower
Single: 110F, Double: 150F, Triple: 210F
Table d'Hôte: 60F per person
Open all year
Good English spoken
Region: Normandy

Jean Masdoumier is a sculptor and former theatre artist who has a great love for his native Limousin countryside. He has converted an old farm complex dating from 1550 into a bed and breakfast which functions also as a small conference centre and a retreat for stress reduction. Monsieur Masdoumier's bed and breakfast enterprise is complemented by his wife Anna's homeopathic medicine practice in an adjoining part of their charming old house. Monsieur Masdoumier has taken great care and pride in renovating the historic building, displaying its lovely stone floors, massive fireplaces and an ancient tower stairway original to the complex. Bedrooms are small and functional, and guests are encouraged to spend time in the public areas. A comfortable, attractively decorated study upstairs leads to the bedrooms and is a cosy room for a relaxing read or chat. Downstairs guests may choose to spend time in the "peasant" salon or the convivial dining room. There is also a wonderful gymnasium in an adjoining converted barn for guests' use and ponies are available for treks in the enchanting countryside. *Directions:* Travel northeast of Limoges approximately 35 kilometers on N20. Turn onto D28 at Bessines. Follow directions for Bersac sur Rivalier and Laurière, turn left after the railroad bridge, then follow arrows to Domaine du Noyer.

DOMAINE DU NOYER
Hosts: Jean and Anne Masdoumier
Bersac sur Rivalier, 87370 St Sulpice Lauvière, France
tel: 55.71.59.54
4 Rooms, all with private shower/WC
Single: 200F, Double 240F
Table d'Hôte: 80F per person
Open March 1 to November 30
Very good English spoken
Region: Limousin

Betschdorf is a picturesque, half-timbered town which has always been known for its distinctive blue-toned stoneware. Traditional pottery methods are handed down from generation to generation, and host Christian Krumeich represents the ninth generation of potters in his family. He and his artistic wife Joelle have installed charming guest quarters above their large pottery workshop, offering independent, stylish accommodation to travellers. Rooms are small yet very attractive, furnished in highly tasteful combinations of contemporary and antique furniture. Artful decor includes pastel upholstery, Monet prints, dried flower arrangements and colourful durrie rugs. The guest salon, decorated with Oriental rugs, antique furniture, well-chosen objets d'art and bookshelves stocked with interesting reading, offers a refined, comfortable ambiance for relaxation and meals. *Directions:* Betschdorf is located approximately 44 kilometers northeast of Strasbourg. Take N63 past Hagenau, continuing on D263 towards Hunspach and Wissembourg. After about 10 kilometers, turn right onto D243 to Betschdorf. Soon after entering town, on the main street, look for the Krumeichs' driveway on the right, marked by a sign for Poterie and Chambres d'Hôtes.

CHEZ KRUMEICH
Hosts: Christian and Joelle Krumeich
23, rue des Potiers
67660 Betschdorf, France
tel: 88.54.40.56
3 Rooms, all with private WC & shower or bath
Double: 200-240F
No Table d'Hôte
Open all year
Some English spoken by Joelle
Region: Alsace

La Grande Métairie, a characterful 16th-century stone farmhouse, belonged to Christine Moy's grandfather.   Happily, very little has been changed except for the necessary modernization for plumbing and electricity.   The beamed-ceilinged dining room is a gem: an enormous fireplace, copper pots, fresh flowers, antique fruitwood side-board and stone floors gleaming with the patina of age and walls three feet thick.   Here Christine sets the table with a checkered table cloth and serves on Limoges china simple, yet superb meals from food almost totally grown on their organic farm - even the butter, meat, cheeses and vegetables come from their property.   There are two tastefully decorated bedrooms plus a 2-bedroom apartment.   La Grand Métairie is a simple working farm, yet the accommodations, ambiance, and genuine warmth of welcome far outshine the modest price (there is even a swimming pool on a back terrace).   *Directions:* Ruffec is located 147 km NE of Bordeaux via the N10.   From Ruffec take D740 east toward Confolens.   After the road crosses the river, take D 197 toward Bioussac.   In 1.3 km turn left toward Oyer.   Soon you will see La Grande Métairie on your left.

LA GRANDE MÉTAIRIE
Hosts: Christine & Jean Louis Moy
Oyer
16700 Bioussac, France
tel: 45.31.15.67
2 Rooms & 1 Apt All with private bath/WC
Double: 200F; 2-bedroom apt 1,800F/week
Table d'Hôte 55F per person
Credit cards: None
Open April 7 through October 31
Swimming pool, bicycles
Fluent English spoken
Region: Limousin

The Chateau de Cheman is a wonderfully enchanting castle dating from the 14th century where Madame Antoine has made her home since 1941. She takes great pride in her historic home and the rose and red wines produced here. The ancient, arched stone entry leads up to circular slate steps, worn by generations of use. Old wooden doors set in the tower stairwell lead into the Antoines' two guest apartments. The first is very spacious, with a sitting room and fully equipped kitchen area: walls and floors are stone, warmed by soft Oriental carpets, tapestries and wallpaper. The bedroom is furnished with elegant antiques and old prints, gilt light fixtures and gold trimmed furniture. A stone archway leads to the bathroom which is thoughtfully stocked with fresh towels, soap, and cottonwool. The second apartment is smaller, but also contains lovely furnishings and has a private terrace. Guests may choose to stay at the Chateau de Cheman either on a bed and breakfast basis, or, for longer stays, at a weekly rate. *Directions:* Blaison is located 15 kilometers east of Angers on the south bank of the Loire. Take D751 to St Jean des Mauvrets, then take D132 through St Sulpice. Look for a hard-to-see sign indicating Chambres d'Hôtes which marks the chateau's long driveway.

CHATEAU DE CHEMAN
Hosts: Madame Alvina Antoine
Blaison Gohier, 49320 Brissac Quince, France
tel: 41.57.17.60
2 Apartments, both w/private bath or shower/WC
Double: 450F, Triple: 650F
No Table d'Hôte
Open all year
No English spoken
Region: Loire Valley

Alain and Francoise Poisot offer very comfortable and stylishly decorated accommodation in their mid-19th-century townhouse. Although located right in the small town of Le Blanc, their gracious house is found in a tree-shaded and landscaped garden ensuring quiet, peaceful surroundings. Monsieur was formerly an interior designer and wallpaper dealer in Paris, thus the interior of their home showcases some beautiful fabrics and wall coverings. Lovely antique paintings, watercolours, plates and furnishings add character to the downstairs salon and dining room, and each bedroom is unique with its own tasteful colour scheme and charming details. Madame is solicitous of her guests' every need and comfort, and supplies bottled water, soap, foaming bath gel and soft, fluffy towels in each room. The Poisots offer two different breakfast options to their guests: the traditional, light French breakfast of coffee and croissants or the more copious "petit dejeuner Varsovie" which also includes eggs, cereal, pastry, fresh or hot fruit and yogurt. *Directions:* Le Blanc is located approximately 60 kilometers east of Poitiers via N151. Once in the village of Le Blanc, follow signs for La Gendarmerie, after which you will see the Poisots' gateposts marked with a Chambres d'Hôtes sign.

LA VILLA VARSOVIE
Hosts: Alain and Francoise Poisot
73, rue de la République
36300 Le Blanc, France
tel: 54.37.29.03
7 Rooms, all with private bath
Single: 285F, Double: 320-370F, Triple: 500F
Table d'Hôte: 100F per person
  (advance notice requested)
Open all year
No English spoken
Region: Limousin/Berry

The Le Quéré family lives in a lovely old manor house dating from the 1700s that is also a working farm. The large, ivy-covered home is set back behind a tranquil green lawn and approached by way of a long, shady drive. The sunny dining room is furnished with tapestry chairs, a long wooden table and a Parisian marble fireplace and is a pleasant place to linger over breakfast. The guest bedrooms all have lovely hardwood floors and harmonious wallpapers, bedspreads and curtains. Most are simply furnished with family antiques and comfortable, contemporary chairs and tables. The three first-floor bedrooms share a common bath and WC, while the two third-floor bedrooms share a communal shower room and WC. The Le Quéres' farm bed and breakfast is not located near any well-known tourist areas, but offers instead tranquil, countryside surroundings providing many opportunities for scenic drives, walks or cycling tours. Guests can experience a true slice of French country life enhanced by a warm welcome and reasonable prices. *Directions:* The Le Quérés' farm is located approximately 40 km north of Limoges. Take N147 to Bellac and then follow N145 in the direction of La Souterraine. After about 1 km, turn left onto a small road across from a John Deere farm machinery dealership. Signs point the way to the Le Quérés' farm.

CHEZ LE QUÉRÉ
Hosts: Monsieur and Madame Le Quéré
Commune de Blanzac; RN 145
Rouffignac, 87300 Blanzac, France
tel: 55.68.03.38
5 Rooms, all share 2 WC/shower/baths
Single: 120F, Double: 165F, Triple 200F
Table d'Hôte: 68-70F per person
Open all year
Good English spoken
Region: Limousin

A mountain road winds through rustic Alpine hamlets and grassy fields of wildflowers to reach the Bertrands' contemporary home. Circular in shape, the house was designed by Monsieur, an architect by trade, and built on a ridge overlooking mountain ranges on either side. Inside, all bedrooms are built around a central living area which has picture windows showing off the lovely view. Floral-print drapes bring a breath of spring into the attractive living area which contains inviting couches and a cosy fireplace. Guest bedrooms are small but comfortable and are accessible either through the Bertrands' living area or via French doors leading out to a garden and tree-covered hillside. Monsieur and Madame Bertrand and their teenaged children are friendly and solicitous hosts who also enjoy sharing home-cooked family meals with their guests. *Directions:* Bois Barbu is located about 30 kilometers southwest of Grenoble. From Grenoble, go through Sassenage, then take D531 to Villard de Lans. Just before the village of Villard de Lans, turn right towards Cote 2000 and Correçon. 1 kilometre later turn right following signs for Bois Barbu and Val Chevrière. At Bois Barbu take the left-hand fork of the road which will climb up slightly. Turn left again just before L'Auberge des Montards, then follow the winding road up to Col du Liorin and look for the Bertrands' low white house on the left.

CHEZ BERTRAND
Hosts: Monsieur and Madame Bertrand
Bois Barbu, 38250 Villard de Lans, France
tel: 76.95.82.67
2 Rooms, both with private sink/WC/share shower
Double: 180F
Demi-pension: 150F per person
Open all year
No English spoken
Region: French Alps

The Bons' romantic Alpine cottage is found high in a meadow filled with wildflowers and bordered by dark pine trees. Dominique and Agnes are a young, attractive couple who have lovingly restored and decorated their 250-year-old farmhouse, adding modern comfort while accenting its rustic country charm. Agnes is a wonderfully creative cook and enjoys preparing healthy, gourmet meals for guests. We enjoyed a friendly meal with the Bons and their three children which featured a crisp green salad, a delicate pork dish made with plenty of fresh eggplant and garden tomatoes, a selection of regional cheeses, and homemade custard topped with ripe strawberries. Upstairs bedrooms are all freshly renovated with dainty flowered wallpapers and matching coverlets, complemented by country antiques and bouquets of field flowers. Rooms are small, but guests are invited to make themselves at home in the pretty downstairs sitting room with a cosy wood stove and well-stocked bookshelves. *Directions:* Bois Barbu is located about 30 kilometers southwest of Grenoble. From Grenoble, go through Sassenage, then take D531 to Villard de Lans. Just before the village of Villard de Lans, turn right towards Cote 2000 and Corrençon. 1 kilometre later turn right following signs for Bois Barbu and Val Chevrière. Continue 3 kilometers and turn left opposite the cross-country ski centre onto the Bons' gravel driveway.

CHEZ BON
Hosts: Agnes and Dominique Bon
Bois Barbu, 38250 Villard de Lans, France
tel: 76.95.92.80
3 Rooms, all with private shower/WC
Single: 190, Double: 220F, Triple: 330
Table d'Hôte: 80F per person
Open all year
Some English spoken
Region: French Alps

Built by monks in the late 1400s to early 1500s, this half-timbered manor house is filled with historic ambiance. Madame Delort has lived here for 45 years and has been hosting travellers since 1978. She obviously loves having personal contact with her guests, but unfortunately speaks no English. We arrived on a damp day in early spring, and were immediately ushered into the dining room to warm our feet beside the large open stone hearth. Breakfast is served at one long table in this atmospheric room framed by half-timbered walls and a beamed ceiling. The country antique furnishings are dominated by a huge chest filled with a colourful collection of old plates. A winding wooden staircase leads to the first floor where Madame Delort's guest rooms can sleep up to five and six people respectively. Bedrooms are not elegant, but they impart an authentic sense of the past, with beautiful original tile floors and antique armoires. Madame Delort's bed and breakfast is a reasonably priced, picturesque base from which to explore the Normandy area. *Directions:* La Boissière is located 8 kilometers west of Lisieux. Take N13 towards Caen, and you will see a Chambres d'Hôtes sign before reaching the town of Boissière which directs you to turn to the left. About 1 kilometre later another sign will indicate a long driveway to the right and you will see this typical Norman manor house set behind a pretty front garden.

CHEZ DELORT
Hostess: Madame Delort
La Boissière, 14340 Cambremer, France
tel: 31.32.20.81
2 Rooms, both with private bath/WC
Single: 145F, Double: 180F, Triple: 230F
No Table d'Hôte
Open April 1 to November 1
No English spoken
Region: Normandy

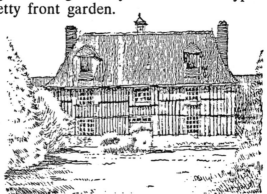

In French, *le tresor* means a treasure, and we decided immediately that Monsieur and Madame Letresor were very aptly named. This attractive couple thoroughly enjoy welcoming travellers into their 450-year-old, half-timbered manor house, and it is not surprising that they have built up a very faithful clientele over the last 15 years. One of their returning guests is a New York artist who visits once a year and stays for a month at a time in order to paint the surrounding countryside: his pretty watercolours are found adorning the walls of the Letresors' home. This home is full of character inside and out, with huge, open-hearthed stone fireplaces in both the salon and breakfast room, complemented by country antique furniture. Upstairs, the bedrooms are also very inviting with stone fireplaces, antique beds and armoires. Our room was the smaller of the two, cosy and intimate with an ancient cupboard door, convenient writing table and window with pretty view of the garden. We have fond memories of the Letresors and their picturesque home and recommend it highly, particularly to those travellers who value authentic charm and a warm welcome over luxurious comfort. *Directions:* Bonnebosq is located about 32 kilometers east of Caen. Two kilometers north of Bonnebosq on D16 look for a Chambres d'Hôtes sign directing you to turn right onto a country road. Another sign marks the Letresors' driveway to the left.

CHEZ LETRESOR
Hosts: Monsieur and Madame Letresor
Manoir du Champ Versant, 14340 Bonnebosq, France
tel: 31.65.11.07
2 Rooms, both with private bath/WC
Single: 150F, Double: 195F, Triple: 255F
No Table d'Hôte
Open April 1 to November 1
Very little English spoken
Region: Normandy

An old stone house dating from 1700 is the site of the Tricketts' intensive language school, translating service and bed and breakfast.   They have renovated the entire house; preserving the old stone walls, large walk-in fireplaces and beamed ceilings. Bedrooms are functional with sparse, yet tasteful furnishings and each has its own very clean shower and sink area.   Dried flower arrangements, dainty Laura Ashley print wallpapers and crocheted lace curtains add charm and warmth to the cool stone architecture.   The Tricketts offer bed and breakfast on a nightly basis or week-long stays combining language programmes with leisure time.   These enjoyable and effective courses are offered at every level and are limited to six persons per class.   Ian and Christiane are from England and France respectively and form an energetic and talented teaching and translating team.   *Directions:* Bourdeilles and the small hamlet of La Rigeardie are located about 24 kilometers northwest of Périgueux.   From Périgueux take D939 towards Brantôme and Angoulême turning left onto D106 following signs for the Chateau de Bourdeilles. Continue through the village of Bourdeilles without crossing the bridge over the river, then turn left onto D78 towards Lisle and Riberac.   After passing the sign for the hamlet of La Rigeardie, the Tricketts' is the first house on the left.

CHEZ TRICKETT
Hosts: Ian and Christiane Trickett
Service de Reservation Loisirs Accueil
16, rue Wilson, 24000 Périgord, France
tel: 53.53.99.99   fax: 53.04.56.95
6 Rooms, all w/private shower/sink, share 2 WC
Single: 160F, Double: 220F, Triple: 250F
Table d'Hôte ONLY available on language week
Open all year
Fluent English spoken
Region: Périgord

This storybook château is actually located in the small town of Port Boulet on the road between Chinon and Bourgueil. Built by the same family who went on to build the well known châteaux Azay-le-Rideaux and Chenonceaux, the Château des Réaux could be out of a fairytale with its twin, red-checked towers and pretty setting. Inside, Madame Goupil de Bouillé establishes a friendly atmosphere and is present to genuinely welcome all her guests. Climb the well-worn turret stairs to the salon where aperitifs are served round a table amidst elegance and comfort. Madame's feminine touch is evident throughout and she has managed to make every room an inviting haven of antiques, paintings, polished silver and authentic memorabilia. Many friendships are made and congenial hours spent in the comfy salons and at the large oval dining table where all the guests may share a meal. The twelve bedrooms in the château and five in a neighboring annex all have private baths and are charmingly decorated with antiques set off by delicate floral print bedspreads, curtains and wallpapers. We look forward to returning to the Château des Réaux, a historical monument that radiates warmth, hospitality and beauty. *Directions:* Travelling south from Bourgueil on D749, turn right immediately after the bridge over the railroad tracks where a sign is posted for the chateau.

CHÂTEAU DES RÉAUX
Hosts: Jean-Luc & Florence Goupil de Bouillé
Le Port Boulet, 37140 Bourgueil
tel: 47.95.14.40 fax: 47.95.18.34
17 Rooms, all w/pvt bath
Double: 490-1000F
Table d'Hôte: 230F per person
Open all year
Good English spoken
Region: Loire Valley

The Moulin Bleu is perched on a scenic vantage point above the Loire Valley, looking out over vineyards and farmlands below.   Round tables with bright blue umbrellas, blue and white checked placemats and napkins dot the flagstone terrace where guests may enjoy breakfast and light snacks throughout the day.   Madame Breton is an energetic and lively hostess who welcomes guests as if they were visiting friends.   The Moulin Bleu (Blue Windmill) actually used to be two old mills side by side, one of which has been converted into Madame's cosy cottage. The two guest bedrooms are furnished with a mix of family antiques and more contemporary furniture, creating a home-like, familial feeling throughout. The windmill next door is still in its original state, and it is here in an wonderful old room with vaulted, stone ceilings that Madame offers winetastings, samplings of pates and cheeses and savoury Table d'Hôte dinners to tour groups and her bed and breakfast guests.   *Directions:* Bourgueil is located 21 kilometers east of Saumur on the north bank of the Loire.   From Saumur, take N147 north in the direction of Longue, then at the roundabout turn right onto D10 (which changes to D35) towards Bourgueil.   Look for signs pointing the way to Le Moulin Bleu to the left - the blue windmill on the hill is visible from afar.

LE MOULIN BLEU
Hostess: Françoise Breton
37140 Bourgueil, France
tel: 47.97.71.41
3 Rooms, all with private bath/WC
Single: 175F, Double: 195F
Table d'Hôte: 65F per person
Open all year
Very little English spoken
Region: Loire Valley

The 200-year-old Domaine de Monciaux, set in well manicured gardens, is positively beguiling - not at all foreboding as some castles can be. The facade is of a creamy tan stone which is softened by white shuttered windows and laced with ivy. Two turrets with peaked slate gray roofs frame the building and add a jaunty, proper French appeal. In the gardens are a pretty swimming pool and tennis court. Inside the castle has many antiques. Some of the furnishings seem a bit fussy, but the dining room is outstanding with a long dining table surrounded tall upholstered chairs. The guest rooms are each individually decorated combining a few antiques with more modern furnishings. The Domaine de Monciaux's greatest appeal is the fairy-tale beauty of the castle and the sincerely warmth and good management of Veronique Alton, the owner's daughter. An added bonus is the excellence of the food prepared by her husband, Philip. *Directions:* Bourrou is located 27 km southwest of Périgeux. Take N21 south from Périgueux for about 23 km. Turn west on D24 toward Villamblard. Go 3 km and turn right. Go through the tiny village of Bourrou and follow signs to Domaine de Monciaux.

DOMAINE DE MONCIAUX
Hosts: Albert Martin & Family
Bourrou
24110 St. Astier, France
tel: 53.81.97.69 fax: 53.80.19.37
8 rooms, all with private bath/WC
Double: 450-600F, Triple: 600-750F
Table d'Hôte: 190F per person
Credit cards: VS
Open March to November
Fluent English spoken
Pool, tennis
Region: Dordogne - Périgord

Monsieur and Madame Pochat are charming and cultivated hosts who welcome guests with enthusiasm and warmth into their lovely, historic home. It was purchased in a state of uninhabited disrepair, but the Pochats have carefully restored the main house, its authentic pigeon tower and nearby outbuildings to form a harmonious ensemble of exposed stone walls and warm tile roofs that look much as they must have when originally built in the mid 1600s. Bedrooms are beautifully furnished in highly polished antiques and decorated with soft-hued fabric wall coverings, old paintings and objets d'art. Details such as fresh fruit and flower bouquets upon guests' arrival are typical of the Pochats' thoughtful and personalized welcome. They are happy to pamper guests by serving breakfast in the rooms and invite all who visit Les Vignes to be seduced by the birdsongs, wildflowers and serenity of the countryside. *Directions:* Brassac is located about 38 kilometers east of Agen. Take N113 in the direction of Moissac, turning left onto D953 at Valence. Continue to the hamlet of Fourquet, turning left onto D7 to Brassac. Go through Brassac, staying on D7 towards Bourg de Visa, and after 3 kilometers turn left onto CV3 towards Le Bugat. Travel 1 kilometre then turn right onto CV10 - the driveway to Les Vignes is about 500 metres farther on the right.

LES VIGNES
Hosts: Monsieur and Madame Pochat
Brassac, 82190 Bourg de Visa, France
tel: 63.94.24.30
2 Rooms & 1 2 bdrm. suite, all w/pvt baths
Double: 230F, Triple/Foursome: 430F
No Table d'Hôte (guest kitchen available)
Open May 1-Oct 1
Good English spoken, also German
Region: Tarn and Garonne

The Chateau de Brélidy is located in central Brittany, in an area surrounded by quiet woods and fishing streams. Monsieur and Madame Yoncourt and their son are the gracious hosts who solicitously attend to their guests' every need. Brélidy is a chateau hotel offering luxurious hotel-type accommodation, and, fortunately for travellers with smaller pocketbooks, the Yoncourts offer more modest bed and breakfast accommodation as well. These guest bedrooms are located up the grand stone staircase on the third floor and were formerly attic rooms. Newly renovated and redecorated, the rooms are not particularly large but are very home-like, comfortable and spotlessly clean. Guests are invited to relax in the castle's salon where tapestry chairs, a huge open fireplace, vases of fresh flowers and objets d'art create a refined setting. A stay here is as comfortable as it is atmospheric, for, although the castle dates from the 16th century, the Yoncourt family has worked hard to restore it to its current polished state of perfection. *Directions:* Brélidy is located approximately 40 kilometers northwest of St Brieuc. From Guingamp, take D8 towards La Roche Derrien, turning left after 11 kilometers onto D15 to Brélidy. Directions to the chateau are well marked once you arrive in the village; thus you need only follow signs for the Chateau de Brélidy.

CHATEAU DE BRÉLIDY
Hosts: Yoncourt Family
Brélidy, 22140 Begard, France
tel: 96.95.69.38 fax: 06.05.18.03
4 Rooms, all with private bath/WC
Double: 295-440F, Triple: 590F
Table d'Hôte: 165F per person; advance notice
Open all year
Very good English spoken
Region: Brittany

Lacy wisteria vines cover the facade of the Coulons' old mill which dates from 1729. The setting is extremely peaceful, next to a cool stream, in the middle of wooded countryside. A stay at the Coulons' could be likened to a visit to one's grandparents' home in the country, and is recommended for those travellers seeking simple accommodation in a quiet, dignified house. Rooms are furnished and decorated in an old-fashioned style and are comfortable and home-like rather than luxurious: most bathrooms are shared. A small upstairs sitting area furnished in family antiques offers guests a cosy spot in which to relax. Breakfast is enjoyed in the downstairs dining room at an intimate round table adorned with a large bouquet of garden flowers. A former bread oven and stone fireplace reflect the history of the room. Located about a two hours' drive from Paris, Chez Coulon is a good choice for a stopover heading south. *Directions:* Briarres sur Essonne is located approximately 35 kilometers southwest of Fontainebleau. Take N152 towards Orleans to the town of Malsherbes and turn left onto D948 to Briarres sur Essonne. Continue 1.5 kilometers past the village and turn off following a small sign towards Francoville, then travel past an old farm to the river where you will see the Coulons' home.

CHEZ COULON
Hosts: Monsieur and Madame Bernard Coulon
Franconville
45390 Briarres sur Essonne, France
tel: 38.39.13.59
2 Rooms, share 1 large bath, separate WC
Single: 150F, Double: 220F, Triple: 260F
No Table d'Hôte
Open April 1 to November 1
No English spoken
Region: Loire Valley

If you want to experience genuine French hospitality in a story-book chateau, the Chateau de Brie is perfection. Do not be intimated by the titles of the owners: Comte and Comtesse du Manoir de Juaye's welcome is so warm, so genuine, that you will feel right at home. The castle was used for many years only for holidays, but now it is the family's permanent home. And, although the four daughters live away, they too love the chateau and come home as often as possible. The rooms of the castle are elegant yet comfortable. The furnishings are gorgeous - all family antiques which have been in the castle forever. One of the most endearing qualities of this castle, is, that although the walls are 2 meters thick, light streams through the many windows giving the rooms a light and airy ambiance. The Chateau de Brie is surrounded by pretty gardens and grassy lawns which stretch out behind the castle to tranquil views of trees and farmland. Beyond the manicured park dominated by the picture-perfect castle, the family owns 1000 acres of forest - a haven for walking. *Directions:* Brie is located 45 km southwest of Limoges. From Limoges go southwest on N21 for 35 km. Exit at Chalus and follow the D 42 west toward Cussac. In about 8 km you will see the Chateau de Brie well signposted on the right side of the road.

CHATEAU DE BRIE
Hosts: Comte & Comtesse Pierre du Manoir de Juaye
Brie, 87150 Champagnac la Riviere, France
tel: 55.78.17.52
4 Rooms, All with private bath/WC
Single: 550-650F, Double: 550-650F, Triple: 750F
Table d'Hôte: 250F per person
Credit cards: None
Open May to November
Fluent English spoken
Region: Limousin

The Chateau de la Bourgonie is absolute perfection combining all the ingredients to make a stay in France unforgettable: fabulous old stone chateau dating back to the 14th-century, breathtaking antiques, stunning decor and a marvelously interesting history.   As if this weren't enough, the owners, Christine and Hubert de Commarque, open their hearts as well as their home to their guests.   The chateau is a quadrangle, built around a large central courtyard.   One wing can either be used as a complete "home" with kitchen, dining room, living room and four bedrooms (perfect for stays of a week or more) or, the four bedrooms are also available on a bed and breakfast basis.   When I asked the charming Christine how long the chateau had been in her family, the answer was very simple "forever". Just a short drive away, perched on a hillside above the Dordogne River, the de Commarque family owns the Chateau de la Poujade, an equally gorgeous home available by rent by the week.   *Directions:* Le Buisson is located 128 km east of Bordeaux.   From Le Buisson take D25 toward Siagrac.   As you leave Le Buisson, take the first road to the right which goes over the railroad tracks and up the hill. When the road splits, go left. The road dead ends at Chateau de la Bourgonie.

CHATEAU DE LA BOURGONIE
Hosts: Christine & Hubert de Commarque
Paleyrac
24480 le Buisson, France
tel: 53.22.01.78
4 Rooms, all with private bath/WC
Double: 700F; 4 bedroom apt 8,000F week
No Table d'Hôte
Credit cards: None accepted
Open May to mid-November
Fluent English spoken
Region: Dordogne

Bed & Breakfast Descriptions

Madame Boyer de Latour lives in her ivy-covered family home which dates from the 1700s. The house has some lovely antique furniture, interesting artifacts and objets d'art from her 20 years of living in North Africa and the Far East while her husband was in the diplomatic service. Old paintings and prints decorate the walls and Oriental rugs cover the handsome wood and tile floors. The house is not luxurious: in fact, if one looks closely it is rather frayed at the edges, yet the elegant furnishings speak of better days gone by. The two guest bedrooms in the main house display some beautiful antique pieces and have private baths. The other two rooms are in an adjoining building and are less appealing. Madame Boyer de Latour appreciates advance reservations for bed and breakfast guests. *Directions:* The Bus St Rémy listing of this bed and breakfast is misleading, since it is actually found closer to the village of Bray et Lu. Travel 56 kilometers northwest of Paris via A15, changing to N14 to Magny en Vexin, then taking D86 to Bray et Lu. In Bray et Lu look for a Chambres d'Hôtes sign directing you to leave the village on D146 towards St Rémy. At the edge of town look for a large gate with a Chambres d'Hôtes sign on it. Be careful not to drive right by, as there is no driveway; the gate is flush with the road.

LA JONQUIÈRE
Hostess: Madame Boyer de LaTour
Le Petit Beaudemont
Bus St Rémy 27630 Ecos, France
tel: 34.67.72.40
4 Rooms, 2 with private shower or bath/WC
Single: 170F, Double: 200F
No Table d'Hôte
Open all year
Very little English spoken
Region: Ile de France

Located in the open countryside south of the Loire Valley, the imposing Chateau du Boisrenault sits in a grove of lush, green trees. Hostess Sylvie Du Manoir is a charismatic hostess who is also a picture framer. She has decorated her guest bedrooms with plenty of artistic flair and sometimes a touch of whimsy, assigning each its own distinctive theme. The informal "Tahitian" room has painted murals of tropical scenes, blue sky and clouds, while the highly traditional "English country" room is an understated blend of lovely antique furniture, rugs and framed prints. All the bedrooms are very tasteful with a strong emphasis on guest comfort. Downstairs public areas are spacious and have lofty high ceilings, yet the Du Manoirs have fortunately managed to maintain a warm, comfortable feeling so that one is not overwhelmed by the sheer size of the rooms. A wood-panelled library offers ping-pong, television and a selection of English books. *Directions:* Buzançais is located approximately 25 kilometers northwest of Chateauroux. Take N143 in the direction of Tours until reaching Buzançais. Once in the village, turn right towards Vierzon on D926 and continue for about 3 kilometers. Look for a large stone cross by the side of the road and a Chambres d'Hôtes sign which directs to the chateau.

CHATEAU DU BOISRENAULT
Hosts: Yves and Sylvie du Manoir
36500 Buzançais, France
tel: 54.84.03.01 fax: 54.84.10.57
6 Rooms, all w/private shower or bath, 3 share WC
Single: 300-340F, Double: 420-430F, Triple: 480F
No Table d'Hôte
Open all year
Good English spoken
Region: Loire Valley

Located in a beautiful area of wooded hills about an hour's drive southwest of Carcassonne is the fabulous 16th-century Chateau de Camon where Dominique du Pont welcomes guests into his home. The picture-perfect chateau (really more like a castle) encloses one side of Camon, a jewel of a walled medieval village which has been designated as one of France's prettiest towns. From the moment you walk into the impeccably groomed inner courtyard, a garden brimming with flowers, you are immersed in the romance of days gone by. This is definitely not the place to take your exuberant youngsters, but rather the kind of elegant retreat to pamper yourself for a few days. Every detail of the castle has been beautifully restored with an eye for perfection. The decor is also delightful with authentic antiques enhancing the fairytale mood of the castle. An added bonus is the beautiful swimming pool - luring guests to linger on summer day, but if you want more more strenuous activities, there is hiking, fishing, or prehistoric caves to explore. *Directions:* Mirepoix is located 47 km southwest of Carcassonne. From Mirepoix go south on D625 for 4 km. Turn east toward Chalabre on D7. In about 10 km you will come to Camon. The chateau dominates the small town - you cannot miss it.

CHATEAU DE CAMON
Hosts: Dominique du Pont
Camon
09500 Mirepoix, France
tel: 61.68.14.05   fax: 61.68.81.56
7 Rooms, all with private bath/WC
Double: 500-1500F
Table d'Hôte: 300F per person
Credit cards: None
Open March to November
Fluent English spoken
Region: Languedoc-Roussillon

A friendly ambiance pervades the Bohics' turn-of-the-century manor house near the port town of Carantec. Perhaps because they share their visitors' love of travel, Monsieur and Madame take great pleasure in welcoming travellers into their home. We were fascinated to hear of their own far-flung adventures in exotic locales such as Brazil, Argentina, Ireland, Israel and the United States. Spend a lazy afternoon exchanging stories on the Bohics' flagstone terrace which looks out over the surrounding artichoke fields to the distant sea. Equally inviting for a chat or a cup of tea is the cosy, antique-filled sitting room where Madame also serves breakfast. Guests are treated to more than just a typical breakfast, as Madame Bohic also offers warm crêpes, fresh croissants and three kinds of homemade preserves. Guest bedrooms all provide a high level of comfort, with fluffy towels, soft sheets and warm blankets. The Bohics' is truly a bed and breakfast where guests are made to feel at home. *Directions:* Carantec is located on the coast approximately 55 kilometers northeast of Brest, 15 kilometers north of Morlaix via D58 in the direction of St Pol de Leon. Turn right onto D173 towards Carantec, and just before entering village look for a Chambres d'Hôtes sign directing you to turn at the first left. Continue to the Bohics' large, grey stone manor house which will be on the right.

KERVEZEC
Hosts: Monsieur and Madame Bohic
29660 Carantec, France
tel: 98.67.00.26
6 Rooms, all w/private bath or shower/WC
Single: 180-220F, Double: 240-280F
No Table d'Hôte
Open all year
Very little English spoken
Region: Brittany

Deep in the enchanted hill country of the Dordogne is an inviting and affordable bed and breakfast. Centuries ago a fortified castle stood on the site where young Patrick Guittard and his parents now raise livestock and produce a local red wine. The old stone farmhouse has been in the Guittard family for three generations: in fact Patrick's grandmother and father were both born in the house. Guest quarters are completely independent and are entered through an oak door off a small flagstone terrace. Guests enjoy breakfast in a modest room whose focal points are a massive, open-hearth fireplace and a lovely view out over the countryside. Patrick has equipped this room with a discreet corner kitchenette plus basic dishes and cooking utensils so that guests may cook their own evening meals if desired. Bedrooms are clean and basic in their furnishings. This is a special place where the simplicity of the accommodation and the fairy-tale quality of the surrounding landscape cast a magic spell from the past. *Directions:* Castang is located about 20 km east of Sarlat. Take D704 from Sarlat in the direction of Cahors, turning left after 3 kilometers onto D704a towards Souillac. At the hamlet of Viviers, turn left towards Castang and keep to the right following signs for Castang. The Guittards' farm complex is the first one on the right.

CHEZ GUITTARD
Host: Patrick Guittard
Castang near Orliaguet, 24370 Carlux
tel: 53.28.84.03
Central Périgeux Reservations: 53.53.99.99
3 Rooms, all share 1 WC, 2 share bath, 1 w/pvt shower
Single: 115F, Double: 130F, Triple: 170F
No Table d'Hôte
Open April to November 30
Very little English spoken
Region: Dordogne

The Chateau du Foulon is an absolute dream: an elegant home surrounded by a 100 acre park complete with 25 handsome peacocks and one naughty swan.   Inside, the rooms without exception are furnished with exquisite family antiques, many dating back to the 17th Century.   The five guestrooms, each beautifully decorated with pretty wallpapers and attractive fabrics, look out over the gardens from large casement windows.   In addition to the five bedrooms, there are also two charming apartments, each with its own little kitchen, bedroom and living room.   The Chateau du Foulon, built in 1840, is the home of Vicomte and Vicomtesse de Baritault du Carpia, who although they do not speak much English, exude a great warmth of welcome.   If you want to explore the Médoc wine region, or just enjoy an interlude in the French countryside, I can think of no lovelier base: this is a place you must plan to stay for a while.   And, one of the happiest surprises is the price which is one of the best values we saw in France.   *Directions:* Take D1 north from Bordeaux for about 28 km.   When you reach Castelnau de Médoc, at the first traffic lights turn left and almost immediately you will see the sign for Chateau du Foulon on your left.

CHATEAU DU FOULON
Hosts: Vicomte & Vicomtesse de Baritault du Carpia
33480 Castelnau de Médoc, France
tel: 56.58.20.18   fax: 56.58.23.43
5 Rooms, all with private bath/WC
Single: 300 F, Double: 350 F, Triple: 450 F
2 one bedroom apartments: 500 F each per night
No Table d'Hôte
Credit cards: None accepted
Open all year
Very little English spoken
Region: Atlantic Coast

A scenic drive through green vineyards and hillsides covered with flaming gorse bushes leads to the village of Le Caylar.   The Clarissacs' grey, two-storey house is found just at the edge of the village, making for quiet, tranquil accommodation. Guest rooms are separate from the main house in an adjoining wing which fronts a shaded garden.   French doors lead from an arched gallery into the peaceful rooms, which the Clarissacs have been offering to travellers for the last 15 years.   The decor is a bit dated, but still attractive, with matching bedspreads and curtains complemented by antiques or reproduction furniture.   On the ground floor of the main house a handsome dining room and lounge is filled with the flavour of days gone by.   Vaulted ceilings and walls are of exposed regional stone, as is the large open-hearthed fireplace.   Country antique furniture, hanging copper pots and dried flower bouquets add warmth and charm, creating a cosy ambiance.   A Table d'Hôte dinner enjoyed here with the Clarissac family is a treat to be long remembered. *Directions:* Le Caylar is located approximately 60 kilometers northwest of Montpellier.   Take N9 through Lodève and continue 18 kilometers towards Millau to Le Caylar.   In the village, turn left just before the restaurant L'Hostellerie du Roc Castel and there will be a sign for Chambres d'Hôtes on the right.

LE BARRY DU GRAND CHEMIN
Hosts: Maryvonne and Bernard Clarissac
34520 Le Caylar, France
tel: 67.44.50.19
5 Rooms, all with private shower/WC
Single: 160F, Double: 200F, Triple: 265F
Table d'Hôte: 85F per person
Open all year
No English spoken
Région: West Provence

Vanessa and John McKeand, a delightful, handsome young couple from England, decided to take a break from their hectic careers as professional musicians and move to the quiet of the French countryside. They bought an old stone farmhouse set in a lovely meadow with a sweeping view over a patchwork of fields fringed by trees and have transformed it into a little jewel. The interior is refreshingly light and airy, reflecting the ambiance of an English cottage. Each room is different, but each is absolutely charming and decorated with antique country furniture and pretty materials which Vanessa has sewn into color coordinated drapes and bed covers. Vanessa and John also operate a small restaurant, very attractively decorated - refreshingly bright and cheerful. In one corner of the dining room is a beautiful harp, a reminder of the days when Vanessa was on the circuit as a professional musician. Now she is the chef, combining the best of English and French cuisine. *Directions:* Chalus is located 35 km southeast of Limoges. Take the N21 southeast from Limoges. At Chalus, turn east following D901 toward Rochechouart. 2.4 km after leaving Chalus, you will a sign for Les Ourgeaux on the right side of the road.

LES OURGEAUX
Hosts: Vanessa & John McKeand
Pageas 87230 Chalus, France
tel: 55.78.50.97 fax: 55.78.54.76
3 Rooms, All with private bath/WC
Single: 265F, Double: 290-345F, Triple 390-445F
Table d'Hôte: 115F per person
Credit cards: MC, VS
Open Easter to November
No smoking, no children under 7
Fluent English spoken
Region: Limousin

Bed & Breakfast Descriptions

Set in the midst of rolling, vineyard-covered hills, the Girards' gracious home offers a wonderful bed and breakfast experience. Formerly a hunting lodge built in 1700, the house is surrounded by grounds and majestic old pine and cedar trees. The ambiance of the Girards' home is one of home-like comfort enhanced by a certain refined elegance. Charming hosts Monsieur and Madame Girard are an attractive couple who delight in making visitors feel right at home. Inviting bedrooms attest to Michelle's flair for decoration, showcasing family antique furniture and harmonious wallpapers, curtains and bedspreads. Details such as bathroom soaps, good bedside lighting, bottled water and sweet-smelling floral print sheets add touches of personalized luxury. Copious breakfasts are served at a long table in the Girards' pretty dining room and include a large bowl of fresh fruits, several different kinds of breads and four varieties of homemade preserves. *Directions:* Chamboeuf is located 18 kilometers southwest of Dijon. Take N74, following signs for Gevrey Chambertin. Turn right in the village of Gevrey onto D31 in the direction of Quemigny Poisot and Chamboeuf. In the village of Chamboeuf, drive to the church and turn left to arrive at the Girard's private car park.

CHEZ GIRARD
Hosts: Monsieur and Madame Girard
21220 Chamboeuf, France
tel: 80.51.81.60
4 Rooms, all with private bath
Single: 250F, Double: 280-300F, Triple: 400F
No Table d'Hôte
Open all year
Very little English spoken
Region: Burgundy

Monsieur and Madame Petit live in an atmospheric 200-year-old cottage covered by thick ivy, tucked away in a tiny country hamlet. Simone is a warm-hearted hostess who offers personal and caring hospitality. She loves plants and nature, and her home is entered through a greenhouse-like hallway festooned with vines and hanging plants. It is easy to feel comfortable and at home in the main sitting room where a cosy fireplace is surrounded by inviting couches and chairs. A bouquet of garden flowers dresses the dining room table where guests gather for breakfast and evening meals. Madame Petit is a creative cook whose breakfasts include several varieties of homemade breads, coffee cake and fruit in addition to the usual Continental fare. Table d'Hôte dinners are relaxed, convivial meals featuring traditional yet healthful country cuisine. Small, charmingly decorated bedrooms offer a high level of comfort with good lighting, bathroom heaters and ample storage space. *Directions:* La Chapelaude is located approximately 10 kilometers northwest of Montluçon. Leave Montluçon on D943 towards Culan then 8 kilometers later, before reaching the town of La Chapelaude, turn right at a service station and follow a country lane to the hamlet of Montroir. The Petits' ivy-covered cottage is one of the first houses on the left.

CHEZ PETIT
Hosts: Monsieur and Madame Petit
Montroir, 03380 La Chapelaude, France
tel: 70.06.45.57
3 Rooms, all with private showers/WC
Single: 140F, Double: 180F, Triple: 190F
Table d'Hôte: 50F per person
Open all year
Very little English spoken
Region: Berry

Madame Eliane Colombet is an interesting and artistic hostess who specializes in making pottery. Her lovely old manor home dates from 1800 and is of stone and plaster construction with red brick decoration. The house is set in an acre of shaded grounds, traversed by the peaceful stream La Chalaronne. Madame offers guest accommodation in a home-like cottage which adjoins her larger house; thus guests are afforded the complete privacy and independence of their own entrance and fully equipped kitchenette. A small, somewhat sparsely furnished salon has a cosy fireplace surrounded by comfortable seating and is decorated with examples of Madame's pottery artwork. Upstairs, the two bedrooms are furnished mostly in antiques and are tastefully decorated with floral print curtains and complementary wallpapers. A shared shower and WC are located on the ground floor. *Directions:* La Chapelle du Chatelard is located approximately 40 kilometers north of Lyon. Take N83 towards Strasbourg and Bourg en Bresse. At Villars les Dombes leave town on D80 towards Beaumont and La Chapelle du Chatelard. Six kilometers after Beaumont, but before the village of La Chapelle du Chatelard, look for a sign for Les Grands Verchères and turn right into Madame Colombet's driveway.

LES GRANDES VERCHÈRES
Hostess: Madame Eliane Colombet
01240 La Chapelle du Chatelard, France
tel: 74.42.85.71
2-bedroom Apartment, share one shower/WC
Single: 250F, Double: 400F, Triple: 560F
No Table d'Hôte
Open all year
Very little English spoken, some German
Region: Burgundy

The Jura region is an unspoilt paradise filled with many lakes, forests, spectacular gorges and rolling, green hills. A nature-lover's delight, the entire department is like one big park preserved in its natural state. Charezier is a small village in the quiet countryside of central Jura near the large lake Vouglans where young Jacqueline and Guy Devenat offer guest accommodation in their spacious, newly remodelled farmhouse. Furnishings are simple and modest, and all is spotlessly clean and well-equipped. Travellers seeking reasonable prices and a relaxed, familial atmosphere will be most at home here, as living quarters are shared with the Devenats and their two small children aged five and seven. Breakfast is informal and is enjoyed in the typical family kitchen. Guy and Jacqueline are friendly and helpful hosts who also put their comfortable living room and television at guests' disposal. *Directions:* Charezier is located approximately 28 kilometers southeast of Lons le Saunier. From Lons, take N78 in the direction of Geneva (Genève) for about 22 kilometers, then turn left onto D27 towards Lake Chalain (Lac du Chalain). After about 4 kilometers, long before reaching the lake, look for a Chambres d'Hôtes sign directing you to turn left to Charezier where the Devenats' contemporary house is easily visible on the left.

CHEZ DEVENAT
Hosts: Jacqueline and Guy Devenat
Charezier, 39130 Clairvaux les Lacs, France
tel: 84.48.35.79
3 Rooms, all with private shower/WC
Single: 100F, Double: 150F, Triple: 170F
No Table d'Hôte
Open all year
No English spoken
Region: Jura

Many farm houses in Provence have been recently purchased, renovated, and turned into bed and breakfasts. These, although they have stylish decor and modern bathrooms, somehow lack the "heart" of the authentic old farms which have been in the same family for many generations. Domaine du Grand Lierne (a large, handsome, stone house with white shutters and tiled roof) has been in the same family for 200 years. The old fashioned interior is a bit dark with papered walls, heavy Napoléon III furnishings, and fine oil paintings, reflecting an aura of elegance and past grandeur. There are three guest rooms. Ask for the large, prettily decorated "Blue Room" upstairs in the main house (the bathroom is down the hall and the toilet downstairs). Even though the modern facilities are not perfect, if you want to step back in time and stay in an immaculately kept farmhouse, you will find at Domaine du Grand Lierne true hospitality and warmth of welcome. Lucette Charignon-Champel, exudes the same "old-fashioned" genuine hospitality as her home. *Directions:* Chateaudouble is located 15 km east of Valence (which is 125 km due north of Avignon). From Valence take D68 east for about 11 km to Chabeuil- continue for about another 4 km to Chateaudouble.

DOMAINE DU GRAND LIERNE
Host: Mme P. Charignon-Champel
Chateaudouble
26120 Chabeuil, France
tel: 75.59.80.71
3 Rooms, 1 with private bath/WC
Single: 150F, Double: 200-250F, Triple: 250-300F
Table d'Hôte: 70F per person
* 1st night only, by prior reservation
Open all year
Some English spoken
Region: Dauphiné/Provence

Set in the green rolling hills and pasturelands of the countryside between the Auvergne and Burgundy regions, the picture-perfect Ferme Auberge de Lavaux combines all the elements for a comfortable and memorable French farm stay. Friendly hosts Paul and Paulette Gelin's farm complex is 150 years old and forms a pretty, tidy ensemble of warm-toned regional stone; carefully renovated to preserve its historic charm. The rustic dining room, originally a stable building, has a cosy atmosphere with exposed stone walls, beams and rafters, and a large stone fireplace. Delicious farm-fresh meals are enjoyed here at long wooden tables adorned with field-flower bouquets. Guest bedrooms are located across the courtyard in a stone annex with a flower-bedecked balcony. Recently remodelled, the bedrooms are all fresh and clean; furnished in antique reproduction furniture and equipped with modern bathrooms. *Directions:* Chatenay is located approximately 55 kilometers west of Macon. Travel on N79 for about 24 kilometers in the direction of Charolles, turning left onto D987 and continuing past Matour to the hamlet of Chevannes where you will turn right onto D300 towards Chatenay. From this point on the route is well-marked with homemade signs for the Ferme Auberge. Follow signs and country roads for about 3 kilometers, through the hamlet of Chatenay, to the Gelins' well-marked driveway.

FERME AUBERGE DE LAVAUX
Hosts: Paul and Paulette Gelin
Chatenay, 71800 La Clayette, France
tel: 85.28.08.48
4 Rooms, all with private WC/bath or shower
Single: 170F, Double: 220F, Triple: 240F
Table d'Hôte: 80-90F per person
Open April 1 to November 15
Very little English spoken
Region: Burgundy

The picturesque medieval town of Beaune is in the heart of the Côte d'Or wine producing district of France. Well known for its gourmet cuisine and fine wines, the region is a popular destination for foreign and French tourists alike, so it is a pleasure to find a good lodging value. Chez Deschamps offers modern comfort, a high level of cleanliness and the independence of hotel accommodation with the warm, personalized atmosphere of a bed and breakfast. Bedrooms are all fresh and new, with thick carpeting, ample closet space, good lighting and spotless private bathrooms. Hostess Marie-Claire Deschamps is a friendly, energetic housewife who thoughtfully provides guests with soap, tissues and even cotton-wool balls, and is happy to help guests plan sightseeing expeditions in the region. Guest accommodation is found in a house completely separate from the Deschamps home and guests have their own home-like breakfast nook and sitting room with full bookshelves and a television. *Directions:* Chorey les Beaune is located about 5 kilometers northeast of Beaune. Take N74 toward Dijon, turning right towards Chorey les Beaune after about 1 kilometre. Just as you enter the village, take the first left and look for a Chambres d'Hôtes sign on the gatepost of the fourth house on the left. The contemporary stucco house in front is the guest house.

CHEZ DESCHAMPS
Hosts: Monsieur and Madame Deschamps
15, rue d'Aloxe-Corton
Chorey les Beaune, 21200 Beaune, France
tel: 80.22.35.59 fax: 80.24.08.01
5 Rooms, all with private shower or bath/WC
Single: 180F, Double: 210F, Triple: 290F
No Table d'Hôte
Open February 1 through December 1
Very little English spoken
Region: Burgundy

Paul and Paulette Hennebel abandoned their successful yet hectic careers in the Paris fashion world 16 years ago to build their dream house in this unspoilt region of central France. Their quaint stone house is surrounded by rolling hills, small lakes and dark pine forests. The Hennebels took great care to build their home in an old style utilizing authentic regional stone and heavy wooden beams. Inside they have created a warm, home-like feeling with Scandinavian natural wood furniture, pretty woven textured fabrics, a large fireplace, full bookshelves and many fresh wildflower bouquets. A well-thought-out floor plan allows guests to enter through a separate entrance which gives access to the two upstairs guest rooms. Furnishings and decor in the bedrooms are fresh and comfortable with much use of natural wood panelling and earth tone colours. The Hennebels are a charming, friendly couple who now cultivate bees and produce honey, bee pollen, honey spice bread and even a delicious liqueur said to have "magic" properties. *Directions:* Cieux is located about 30 kilometers northeast of Limoges. Take N147 to D711 to Cieux. Continue through the village of Cieux on D711 in the direction of St Junien, then turn right following signs for "Circuit des Monts de Blond" and Boscartus to the right. The Hennebels' driveway is a bit farther on the right and is marked with a small yellow sign saying "Miel des Monts de Blond".

CHEZ HENNEBEL
Hosts: Paul and Paulette Hennebel
Les Hauts de Boscartus, 87520 Cieux, France
tel: 55.03.30.63
2 Rooms, both w/shower and sink, share WC
Single: 160F, Double: 200F, Triple: 275F
Table d'Hôte: 100F per person
Open all year
Very little English spoken
Region: Limousin

Madame Bruère has raised five children in her large, turn-of-the-century home and is now happy to fill her spare bedrooms with bed and breakfast travellers. The three-storey stone house is located in a small town   convenient to shops and a train station. Madame has some lovely antiques on display throughout her home, particularly in the dining/breakfast room which is completely furnished in Henry IV style, including table, chairs and sideboard. Large windows let in sunlight and garden flowers lend a fresh, summery feeling. A highly polished, wide wooden stairway leads up to the guest bedrooms, which are located on the second and third floors. Rooms are comfortable, not luxurious, and adequately furnished with family antiques. A stay here under Madame Bruère's motherly wing is rather like making a visit to Grandmother's house; indeed Madame informed us that she already has seven grandchildren. *Directions:* Cinq Mars la Pile is located approximately 22 kilometers west of Tours on the north bank of the Loire. Take N152 in the direction of Langeais and, once in the village of Cinq Mars la Pile, follow signs for Gare SNCF (train station) and Chambres d'Hôtes. The Bruère home is a three-storey house built in 1912.

LA MEULIERE
Hosts: Monsieur and Madame Bruère
10, rue de la Gare
37130 Cinq Mars la Pile, France
tel: 47.96.53.63 or 47.48.37.13
5 Rooms, 3 with private shower/WC
  Other rooms share 1 bath/WC
Single: 160F, Double: 220F, Triple: 260F
No Table d'Hôte
Open all year
No English spoken
Region: Loire Valley

The graceful Chateau de Thoré was once the hunting lodge of Diane de Poitiers, favourite mistress of King Henry II. Down-to-earth hostess Dr Eckels has filled the house with precious objets d'art, Oriental rugs and treasured antique furniture, creating an elegant and stylish home. A stay here offers a rare chance to step back in time to the 16th and 18th centuries, surrounded by all the accoutrements of an aristocratic lifestyle, and experience life in a French castle. The three guest suites are expensive, but all have luxuriously modern private baths and small private sitting rooms. Furnishings are period antiques in impeccable condition, providing both historic atmosphere and creature comfort. The lovely back garden is a peaceful place to enjoy breakfast or evening aperitifs while looking out over an expanse of lawn dominated by several majestic old trees. *Directions:* Civray de Touraine is located right next to Chenonceaux, about 24 kilometers southeast of Tours. The Chateau de Thoré is on the opposite bank of the river from the town of Civray de Touraine. From Chenonceaux, cross the bridge over the Cher River and travel in the direction of Bléré on N76. After 3 kilometers, turn left to the Chateau de Thoré.

* CHATEAU DE THORÉ
Host: Dr Eckels
Allee du Chateau 2
Civray de Touraine, 37150 Bléré, France
tel: 47.23.94.95
3 Suites, all with private bath
Double: 800F
No Table d'Hôte
Open April 1 to October 30
Some English spoken, fluent German
Region: Loire Valley

For a stately 18th-century chateau with sophisticated charm, the Chateau de Barry, is a real winner - especially if you appreciate lovely decor. Here you will find large elegant lounges and seven exceptionally attractive bedrooms. Each is beautifully furnished in antiques and elegant fabrics color coordinating with pretty wall papers. What a surprise to learn that all the sewing for the handsome draperies was done by Mme Bouet who previously was a designer in Paris. Francois Bouet is not only a most talented seamstress, but also a gourmet cook who with previous arrangements will prepare dinner, exquisitely served with fine china and beautiful linens. Chateau Barry is not the family home of the Bouets, but bought by them when M Bouet returned from the Orient. The home beautifully reflects his 35 years in the Far East - many artifacts and furniture of fine quality which he collected during his travels are seen throughout the house, especially in the lounge that overlooks the pool. *Directions:* Clairac is located 125 km southeast of Bordeaux. Take the A62/E72 southeast from Bordeau for about 100 km. Take the Aiguillon exit and follow signs to Aiguillon. Go north on D666 and take the Clairac turnoff. Go across the river, make a jog to the left and follow the road toward Grateloup. When the road splits, go straight and follow Chateau de Barry signs.

CHATEAU DE BARRY
Hosts: M & Mme Rene Bouet
47320 Clairac, France
tel:53.84.35.49 fax: 53.84.35.06
7 Rooms, all with private bath/WC
Double: 500-750F
Table d'Hôte: 300-350F per person
Credit cards: None
Open From May to October
Very little English spoken
Region: Lot and Garonne

Monsieur and Madame Élies' modest, half-timbered cottage is a former cider press-house located on a pretty country lane in the Norman countryside. The guest rooms are located in a separate wing where apples were once crushed in a huge vat. Furnishings are contemporary, but historic atmosphere is provided by the heavy old ceiling beams which were left intact during the renovation process. Each private bathroom is very clean and well-equipped with plenty of towels. Breakfast is served either in the Élies' home-like family room where decor is provided by family photos and knicknacks, or outside on the small terrace. The Élies speak no English, but have two sons aged 12 and 17 who are learning it in school. This small, home-like bed and breakfast is ideal for travellers seeking quiet, comfortable accommodations in beautiful pastoral surroundings. *Directions:* Clarbec is approximately 38 kilometers east of Caen. The easiest route is to turn off N175 approximately 3 kilometers out of Pont L'Éveque onto the bridge which crosses the autoroute. You are now on D280 which will lead you to Clarbec where you should turn onto D285 towards St Hymer. After crossing three little bridges, turn right and look for a sign indicating Chambres d'Hôtes on a gate in front of the Élies' half-timbered cottage.

PESSOIR DU LIEU HUBERT
Hosts: Monsieur and Madame Guy Élie
Lieu Hubert, Chemin de la Galoche
14130 Clarbec, France
tel: 31.64.90.89
1 Room with private bath/WC
Single: 150F, Double: 200F
No Table d'Hôte
Open all year
No English spoken
Region: Normandy

A half-timbered exterior, overflowing windowboxes and a wheelbarrow full of flowers in the front yard of this 250-year-old farmhouse only hint at the country charm found inside. Madame Anfrey is an energetic farmwife who, when not bustling about making sure her guests feel at home, helps her husband tend their cows and poultry. Madame's artistic nature is evident in the very cosy and pleasantly cluttered feeling she has achieved throughout her farm cottage. The guest bedrooms are all charmingly decorated with a variety of antiques, dried flower arrangements and old paintings. Breakfast is served at a round table in the main room supervised by an old grandfather clock in the corner. The low, beamed ceilings, hanging copper pots, country antiques and cosy fire on rainy days make this a tempting spot to linger over cafe au lait, tea or hot chocolate served in country pottery. We were sad indeed to leave this quaint, friendly bed and breakfast. *Directions:* Conteville is located approximately 60 kilometers west of Rouen via A13 to the Beuzeville exit, then N175 to N178 to Foulbec, then D312 to Conteville. There are several Chambres d'Hôtes advertised by roadside signs in the vicinity of Conteville, so be sure to follow those which indicate Le Clos Potier. The route involves several turns, but is very well signposted, and you will find the farmhouse tucked away on a country road behind a white fence.

LA FERME DU PRESSOIR
Hosts: Pierre and Odile Anfrey
Conteville, 27210 Beuzeville, France
tel: 32.57.60.79
3 Rooms, 2 with private bath/WC
Single: 175F, Double: 190F
Table d'Hôte: 100F per person
Open all year
Very little English spoken
Region: Normandy

The Chauveaus are antique dealers who have seasoned their expertise and good taste with a touch of whimsy to create wonderfully imaginative decor and furnishings in their 250-year-old home.   Do not expect to see the same antique pieces on a second visit, however, as Monsieur Chauveau is fond of pointing out that all furniture is for sale and therefore subject to change.   We stayed in a charming attic room with beautiful exposed support beams and an adjoining immaculate bathroom thoughtfully stocked with ample toiletries and luxurious fluffy towels.   Floor level windows overlook the prettily landscaped swimming pool.   The WC is located downstairs, but is private to the room.   Another bedroom is feminine, light and airy, with windows that afford a peaceful view of the surrounding valley and vineyards.   The Chauveaus pay great attention to detail and serve an elegant breakfast complete with gold-trimmed china, silver service and a white linen tablecloth.   Contented appetites are assured after beginning the day with an artful display of exotic fruits, warmed croissants, fresh bread, homemade preserves, rich cheese and country butter.   *Directions:* Cravant les Coteaux is located 8 kilometers east of Chinon.   Take D21 through Cravant les Coteaux in the direction of Panzoult.   Two kilometers after leaving Cravant, look for a sign advertising Pallus, Bernard Chaveau and then take the next driveway on the right.

DOMAINE DE PALLUS
Hosts: Bernard and Barbara Chauveau
Pallus, Cravant les Coteaux, 37500 Chinon, France
tel: 47.93.08.94   fax 47.98.43.00
3 Rooms, all with private bath/WC
Single or double: 500, Triple: 600F
No Table d'Hôte
Open all year
Fluent English, German spoken by Madame
Region: Loire Valley

Crillon le Brave, a walled hilltop village, is comprised of a pretty small church and a cluster of weathered stone houses. One of these houses, the Clos St Vincent, has been completely renovated and is now a delightful bed and breakfast. Guests enter through large iron gates into a spacious parking area in front of a typical tan stone building with brown shutters and tiled roof. A large swimming pool on the terrace captures a sweeping view of the surrounding countryside. There is a very attractive lounge for guests with white-washed walls, tiled floors, a snug nook with a few comfortable chairs for reading, and a large wooden table for dining. The five bedrooms are all very similar in decor with tiled floors, small table and chairs, and color-coordinated, Provençal-style fabrics used as dust ruffles, chair cushions and drapes. The feeling is very fresh, uncluttered, and pretty. *Directions:* Carpentras is located 24 km northeast of Avignon. From Carpentras take D 974 NE toward Bedoin. After about 10 km, follow the road signs to Crillon le Brave. As the road climbs the hill toward the old village, you will see the sign for Clos St. Vincent. Turn right at the sign and continue on a small road for about 200 meters. Turn left and continue up the hill. The Clos St. Vincent is the second driveway on the left.

CLOS ST. VINCENT
Host: Francoise Vazquez
Les Vergers
84110 Crillon le Brave, France
tel: 90.65.93.36
5 Rooms, all with private bath/WC
Single: 260-310F, Double: 290-340F, Triple: 410F
Table d'Hôte: 100F per person
Credit cards: None
Open March to November 15
No English spoken
Region: Provence

The Ricquarts' comfortable home in a former mill enjoys a quiet, pastoral setting in the hilly countryside of Provence.   They are an interesting, well-travelled couple who purchased the mill when it was virtually in ruins and completely remodelled it into the attractive home it is today.   Monsieur is a former officer in the French Air Force, so they have resided in such exotic locales as Egypt, Israel, Morocco and Germany.   Art and artifacts from their overseas journeys complement the contemporary furnishings and decor of the guest bedrooms.   The bedrooms have a high level of comfort and privacy; the bathrooms are clean and modern and there is an independent entrance for guests. The Ricquarts' warm, friendly welcome, reasonable prices and tranquil setting make the Moulin d'Antelon a delightful base from which to explore the historic towns and vividly coloured landscapes of northern Provence.   A large swimming pool has recently been completed. *Directions:* Crillon le Brave is located approximately 9 kilometers northeast of Carpentras.   Take D974 following signs for Le Mont Ventoux par Bedoin.   After travelling about 12 km, 1 km PAST the turnoff for Crillon-le-Brave, look for the Riquart's driveway on the left.   Look carefully, as the house sits below the level of the road.   The driveway is marked with a large sign: Chambres d'Hôtes, Bed and Breakfast.

MOULIN D'ANTELON
Hosts: Bernard and Marie-Luce Ricquart
Crillon le Brave, 84410 Bedoin, France
tel: 90.62.44.89
4 Rooms, both with private bath
Single: 230F, Double: 270F, Triple: 320F
No Table d'Hôte
Open all year
Good English spoken
Region: Provence

The old mill of Chateaubrun is found in a wooded hollow on the banks of the tranquil River Creuse. It is looked after by young Emanuelle Daout who also manages the adjoining wing where wedding receptions, parties and baptisms are catered for. Guest bedrooms are all accessible from a central upstairs landing and share a common bath and WC. Newly renovated, the rooms are all freshly painted and wallpapered and spotlessly clean with soft pastel colour schemes and contemporary light pine furniture. The small rooms have sloping ceilings and windows which let in plenty of sunlight. The downstairs breakfast room is informal and simply furnished in a home-like style. The Creuse Valley is a lovely region, rarely visited by overseas tourists, which remains in its natural wooded state. The Moulin de Chateaubrun is recommended for travellers who like to explore little known areas and who are seeking basic, clean accommodation at reasonable prices. *Directions:* Cuzion is located 52 kilometers south of Chateauroux. Travel on N20 to Argenton sur Creuse, then follow signs for Eguzon via D913. At Eguzon, go left towards Pont des Piles and Orsennes. After about 2 kilometers, turn to the left onto a narrow, tree-shaded road towards Cuzion. Before reaching the village, follow signs to Chateaubrun which lead down to the mill at the river's edge.

MOULIN DE CHATEAUBRUN
Host: Mademoiselle Emanuelle Daout
36190 Cuzion, France
tel: 54.47.46.40
4 Rooms, none with private bath
Single: 100F, Double: 150F
No Table d'Hôte
Open all year
No English spoken
Region: Limousin

Madame de Saint-Père lives in a marvellous old house in the village of Dangu. She speaks fluent English and takes great pleasure in helping her guests plan sightseeing excursions in the surrounding countryside. Her house dates from around 1700, yet her two guest bedrooms are comfortable in size (not always the case in old houses) and are reached by a stairway which is independent of the rest of the house. The decor is an artfully conceived melange of antiques, old etchings and pleasing colour schemes. In one of the rooms the bed is found behind a pretty flowered curtain; an intimate, delightfully French touch. Downstairs there is a cosy salon with a fireplace where guests are invited to relax with an aperitif before enjoying a lively Table d'Hôte dinner with Madame de Saint-Père. Breakfast is often served under a canopy on the terrace, which has a peaceful view over Madame's well-tended garden leading down to the shady banks of the river Ept. A strategically placed bench provides a tranquil spot for an afternoon of reading or quiet contemplation. *Directions:* Dangu is located 60 kilometers northwest of Paris via A15, changing to N14 to Bordeaux St Clair, then D146 to Dangu. In Dangu, look for a green and yellow Chambres d'Hôtes sign directing you to a cream-coloured house with green shutters, located just next to the bridge over the stream.

LES OMBELLES
Hostess: Madame Poulain de Saint-Père
4, rue de Gue, 27720 Dangu, France
tel: 32.55.04.95
2 Rooms, one with private bath/WC
Single: 180F, Double: 250F
Table d'Hôte: 110F per person
Open all year
Fluent English spoken
Region: Normandy

Windowboxes full of multi-coloured flowers decorate the pretty, welcoming facade of Colette Geiger's chalet-style house. She is a friendly, motherly hostess who keeps her home and guest rooms in spotless condition, with pretty, feminine touches such as lace-trimmed pillowcases and sheets. Furnishings are antique reproductions and rooms are small, but very comfortable. Guests are encouraged to relax in the sitting room which is cosy and inviting and has a stone fireplace flanked by leather chairs and picture windows looking out over distant hills. Chez Geiger is found in a beautiful valley dotted with small villages and fields of cherry trees. This is a region of kirsch production and each town has its own distillery where the "water of life" is made from locally grown cherries. *Directions:* Dieffenbach au Val is located approximately 30 kilometers northwest of Colmar. Take N83 towards Strasbourg, turning left at Selestat onto N59 towards St Die. After 3 kilometers, turn right onto D424 towards Ville. At the village of St Maurice turn left following signs for Dieffenbach. Take the next left and then look for a Chambres d'Hôtes sign marking the Geigers' chalet-style house, which is set back from the road behind a front garden.

CHEZ GEIGER
Hostess: Madame Colette Geiger
19, Route de Neuve Eglise
67220 Dieffenbach au Val, France
tel: 88.85.60.48
3 Rooms, all with private shower
Single: 140F, Double: 180F, Triple: 230F
No Table d'Hôte
Open all year
No English spoken, fluent German
Region: Alsace

Les Charmettes is a historic stone house dating from 1781, located on the banks of the tranquil Orleans canal. Hostess Madame Sicot is exceedingly proud of her home which has been in her family for the last 100 years, and is in the process of restoring it to its former beauty. She has a certain flair for decoration and has created a lovely country-home feeling with attractive colour schemes, pretty wallpapers, polished antiques and objets d'art. Two charming and intimate guest bedrooms are found in the former attic servants' quarters at the top of a steep old wooden staircase. The three first-floor bedrooms are more easily accessible and are elegantly decorated with lovely old furniture and collectibles. A peaceful back garden bordering the canal offers a quiet refuge after a day of travel or sightseeing, and is also a pleasant spot to enjoy Madame Sicot's traditional Continental breakfast. *Directions:* Donnery is located approximately 10 kilometers east of Orléans. Take N60 in the direction of Chateauneuf sur Loire and Montargis, turning left onto D709 towards Donnery. Go through the village, turning right at the church following signs for Fay aux Loges. The Sicots' house is not marked with any signs, but is not too difficult to spot as it is the last house on the right along the canal.

LES CHARMETTES
Hosts: Monsieur and Madame Sicot
45450 Donnery, France
tel: 38.59.22.50
5 Rooms, 3 w/private bath, others share
Single: 180F, Double: 250F, Triple: 320F
Table d'Hôte: 100F per person
Open all year
Some English spoken
Region: Northeast Loire

Dating from 1846, Madame Lefloch's ivy-covered manor house is a home-like bed and breakfast, certainly not elegant, but a good choice for families.   Madame is a friendly, very down-to-earth hostess who is happy to share her Brittany crêpe recipes and has prepared a guest book filled with brochures, maps and information on local sights and activities.   Her entry salon is sparsely furnished with country antiques and fresh flower arrangements from her garden.   She loves the feeling of a cosy fire, and at the slightest hint of a chill in the air sets a warm blaze in the old stone fireplace.   The adjoining breakfast room is light and airy, with a charming wooden floor and more old furniture.   On warm mornings guests may also elect to enjoy their breakfast on the sunny terrace overlooking the front lawn.   The guest bedrooms are furnished in a mix of antiques and more contemporary pieces, with some leftover familial touches such as large cartoon drawings on a bedroom wall. *Directions:* Pouldavid is located just south of Douarnenez, which is about 22 kilometers northwest of Quimper via D765.   Just outside of Douarnenez there is a roundabout; continue on D765 towards Audierne.   After the trafficlight, look for a Chambres d'Hôtes sign directing you to turn to the right.   Continue following signs to the Lefloch manor house.

MANOIR DE KERVENT
Hostess: Madame Lefloch
Pouldavid, 29100 Douarnenez, France
tel: 98.92.04.90
4 Rooms, all w/private shower, all share 1 WC
Single: 150F, Double: 190F, Triple: 250F
No Table d'Hôte,
   Crêpe dinners & some cooking facilities
Open all year
Very little English spoken
Region: Brittany

Hélène and Vincent Malo are a young couple who welcome guests to their farm with enthusiasm and warmth. They have 5 independent guest rooms in a former outbuilding. Proud of their Norman heritage, Hélène and Vincent took great care while remodelling to retain the charm of the original building. Inside, a freshness and simple charm is felt throughout the bedrooms, all of which are equipped with a basic sink and shower. The furnishings consist of light pine beds, writing tables and chairs. Lighting is good, and pretty touches such as watercolours by regional artists, lace bonnets and fresh flowers brighten the somewhat sparse decor. Dinners and breakfasts are served in the Malos' airy dining room looking out through picture windows to the front garden. Guests who dine at the Malos' are treated to a homemade pear aperitif, homemade apple cider and deliciously light meals featuring farm and garden produce, all complemented by lively conversation. The Malos are a friendly, accommodating couple who speak enough English to get by very well with their English-speaking guests. *Directions:* Écrainville is located about 25 kilometers northeast of Le Havre via D925 to Goderville, then D139 to Écrainville. In Écrainville take the first right following the sign for Fongueusemare. The Malos' home is 2 kilometers on the right.

LA FORGE VIMBERT
Hosts: Hélène and Vincent Malo
76110 Écrainville, France
tel: 35.27.17.97
5 Rooms, all with sink/shower, all share 2 WC
Single: 180F, Double: 230F, Triple: 280F
Table d'Hôte: 60F per person
Open March 1 through January 1
Good English spoken
Region: Normandy

Dominating the unspoiled medieval village of Entrecasteaux is the Chateau d'Entrecasteaux, a handsome 11th-century castle that is open to the public as a museum, and, for a lucky few who make reservations in advance, as a bed and breakfast. The castle was purchased in the mid-1970's by Ian McCarvie-Munn, a dashing Scotsman whose zest for living and international escapades filled his days with a novel-worthy set of adventures. He was also an exceptionally talented artist and it seems he bequeathed his love of the arts along with his castle to his hospitable son, Lachlan. Lachlan and his wife are patrons of the arts and attract world class exhibits which are beautifully presented in the spacious, sun-lit rooms on the first two floors of the castle which serve as an art gallery, museum and gift shop. One of the guest rooms (a suite brimming with antiques, including an ornate bed, and with a giant marble bathroom) is actually on display during the day as part of the museum. A private staircase leads to the third level where there are two more extremely large guest rooms, light and airy, with high arched windows that offer pretty views of the old town. *Directions:* Entrecasteaux is located approximately 25 km northwest of Brignoles. From Brignoles, take D562 northeast toward Carcès; 3 km beyond Carcès turn north on D31 to Entrecasteaux. The castle is in the middle of the town.

CHATEAU D'ENTRECASTEAUX
Hosts: Mr & Mrs Lachlan McGarvie-Munn
83570 Entrecasteaux, France
tel: 94.04.43.95 fax: 94.04.48.46
3 Rooms, all with private bath/WC
Single: 750F, Double: 750-1500F
No Table d'Hôte
Open all year
Fluent English, Spanish & German spoken
Region: Côte d'Azur

Isabelle and Patrick Blanc are an attractive and extremely energetic young couple who designed and built their rustic-style Auberge d'Anais (named after their adorable little girl) as a complement to their wine-growing activities.   They love to meet people and entertain, and foster an informal, friendly atmosphere where guests feel right at home and friends and family always feel comfortable dropping by.   Their property is set on a vineyard-covered hillside, surrounded by woods and valleys, and ablaze with the graceful yellow jenet flowers in the spring and summer months.   Three guest rooms open out onto an upstairs terrace which overlooks the crystal blue swimming pool, a welcome refuge in this hot, dry climate.   Rooms are Spartanly furnished, but very comfortable and clean, with cool tile floors and modern baths or showers.   Family-style dinners featuring fresh products from the Blancs' nearby farm are served downstairs in the spacious dining room furnished in country antiques.   *Directions:* The village of Entrechaux is located approximately 16 kilometers north of Carpentras via D938 past Malaucene turning right towards St Marcellin les Vaison and then taking the left fork towards Faucon.   Two kilometers later look for a driveway on the left marked with a Chambres d'Hôtes sign as well as a small homemade sign for L'Auberge d'Anais.

AUBERGE D'ANAIS
Hosts: Isabelle and Patrick Blanc
Quartier Peyreras, 84340 Entrechaux, France
tel: 90.36.20.06 or 90.46.02.07
5 Rooms, all w/pvt WC/shower or bath
Single: 190F, Double: 250F, Triple: 310F
Table d'Hôte: 80-130F per person
Open January 1 through November 1
No English spoken
Region: Provence

A stay with the friendly Chaix family on their working farm offers a real taste of rural life in France. Sheep, goats, dogs, cats, chickens and roosters fill the farmyard, but Marcel Chaix's principal occupation is irrigating his soyabean, sunflower, wheat and corn crops. A relaxed, very fun-loving family, Marcel, Madeleine and their four daughters extend a sincere, open-armed welcome. Guest accommodations are found in renovated farm buildings away from the Chaixes' main house, so quiet and privacy are assured. Bedrooms are very clean and basic with contemporary furnishings, although some have exposed stone walls which add historic atmosphere. A well-equipped kitchen is available for guests who wish to cook their own dinner or store picnic supplies during their stay. For travellers seeking simple comfort and warm hospitality in a countryside setting, La Mare is a perfect stopping place. *Directions:* Étoile is located approximately 9 km south of Valence. If arriving from Lyon via autoroute A7, exit at the south Valence exit (Valence Sud), and then follow signs for Gap on D111. At the entry to the village of Étoile, turn left towards Montmeyran. Follow signs advertising Chambres d'Hôtes to arrive at the Chaix farm about 3 km later.

LA MARE
Hosts: Marcel, Madeleine and Nathalie Chaix
Quartier la Mare
26800 Étoile sur Rhône, France
tel: 75.59.33.79
8 Rooms, 5 w/pvt shower/WC, others share
Single: 90-120F, Double: 160-190F, Triple: 195-265F
Table d'Hôte: 60F
Open all year
Very little English spoken by daughters
Region: Rhône Valley

Any doubts that the Mas Poli is very old are quickly dispelled when the personable Christiane Poli shows you the signs of the revolution, a cross and a fleur de lys, carved into the wall of the front of the house.   When Robert and Christiane bought the house 15 years ago it was almost in total ruin: no running water, no heat, holes in the roof.   The characterful old pump still stands in the entry hall, a reminder of the past, as does the old stone horse trough in the living room which used to be the stables but is now a charming, comfortable room where meals are served on chilly days.   Mme Poli has tastefully renovated and decorated all the rooms, maintaining their old world charm while making them comfortable for her guests.   Although the rooms are small, they are meticulously tidy and each decorated with a smattering of antiques and pretty fabrics.   For a budget priced place to stay, the Mas Poli offers great value without sacrificing charm.   *Directions:* Eyragues is located 12 km south of Avignon.   In Eyragues go to the center of the village and follow signs north toward Chateaurenard.   Before leaving town, you come to a Shell station and a "pharmacie".   Take the road to the right of the "pharmacie" and go straight, past 2 stop signs and after about 1.5 km the Mas Poli is on your left.

MAS POLI
Hosts: Christiane & Robert Poli
Chemin des Prés
13630 Éyragues, France
tel: 90.94.19.71
3 Rooms, None with private bathroom
Single: 150 F Double: 200 F, Triple: 300 F
No Table d'Hote
Credit cards: None accepted
Open from April to September
No English spoken (but understood)
Region: Provence

The road seems to end at the tiny mountain hamlet of Freissinières, and one has the feeling of being at the edge of civilization. The village is extremely quiet, and is located on the boundary of the Parc National des Écrins (literally translated, "Jewel Box National Park"). The Relais des Vaudois is a rustic inn run mainly by Madame Moutier. Copious family-style lunches and dinners are served in the charming restaurant which has low, vaulted ceilings and is decorated with country antiques, old farm implements and dried flower arrangements. Bedrooms are very basic, but all are adequately furnished and have private shower and WC. The majority of the rooms have French doors that open onto a sunny front balcony overlooking the village. The Relais des Vaudois is a simple country inn rather than a family home, and is thus recommended mainly as a base for hikers or as an atmospheric lunch stop. *Directions:* Freissinières is located 20 kilometers southwest of Briançon. Take N94 in the direction of Gap. Just before entering the village of La Rôche de Rame, turn right onto D38 to Freissinières, following the road up a lovely valley into the hamlet. Continue through on the narrow street to the T intersection at the end of the village. The Relais des Vaudois is on the right and easy to find.

LE RELAIS DES VAUDOIS
Hosts: Monsieur and Madame Moutier
Freissinières, 05310 La Rôche de Rame, France
tel: 92.20.93.01
12 Rooms, all with private shower
Single: 202F, Double: 224F
Table d'Hôte: 64F per person
Open all year
No English spoken
Region: French Alps

If you are looking for a chateau whose decor is primly perfect, the Chateau de Garrevaques would not be your cup of tea.   But, if you are looking for a warm welcome, this home truly has "heart".   Since the 15th Century, the chateau has been in the family of the charming Mme Barrande who was persuaded by her daughter, Marie-Christine, to open her home as a bed and breakfast.   (In fact, the creative Marie-Christine originated the concept of chateaux in France inviting paying guests.)   Although their jobs dictate they must travel, when in town Marie-Christine (a purser for Air France) and Marie-Christine's husband, Claude Combes (a commercial pilot), live at the chateau.   The whole family exudes genuine hospitality.   If you have heard the French are aloof, a visit to Chateau de Garrevaques will quickly dispel that myth - even the cat (Fish) and the dog (Chips) are super friendly.   Stay here and become friends with a French family.   Dinner is great fun - filled with tales of the chateau (ask about the baby born in prison during the revolution who later retrieved his heritage or the faithful gardener who rescued the castle from destruction by the Nazis).   *Directions:* From Toulouse take D1 southeast for 53 km to Revel.   Turn northeast on D 79F for 5 km to Garrevaques.

CHATEAU DE GARREVAQUES
Hosts: Andrée Barande & Marie Christine Combes
81700 Garrevaques, France
tel: 63.75.04.54 fax: 63.70.26.44
12 Rooms, 8 doubles with private bath/wc
2- 2bedroom suites each share a bathroom
Single: 400F, Double: 650F, Triple: 900F
Table d'Hôte: 170F
Credit cards: AX, VS
Open March 15-November 30 (winter-groups only)
Good English spoken
Region: Tarn

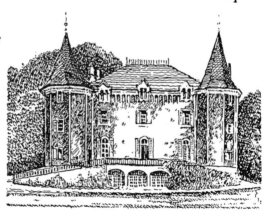

It is a short walk through grassy fields to the sea from this wonderful 17th-century manor house. Francois and Agnes Lemarie are a friendly young couple who, along with their three adorable children aged 5 to 10, enjoy welcoming bed and breakfast guests to their working farm. A strong sense of the past prevails inside the old stone walls of the Lemaries' home, in the adjoining 15th-century chapel, converted to a salon for "discussion, dreaming and listening to music", and in the large stone dovecote in the courtyard. The circular room with hundreds of former pigeon niches provides a unique ambiance for guests to enjoy picnics or light meals. Guest bedrooms are basic, and furnishings vary from very simple to family antiques. Dried flower bouquets warm the somewhat cool stone rooms. Breakfast is served in the Lemaries' dining room reminiscent of days gone by, with its walk-in stone fireplace and hanging copper kettle, heavy beamed ceiling and old farm furniture. *Directions:* Géfosse is located approximately 30 kilometers northwest of Bayeux. Take N13 west just past St Germain du Pert, then D514 north towards Grandcamp Maisy. Turn left onto D199A to Géfosse. There are roadside signs for more than one Chambres d'Hôtes so be sure to follow those marked L'Hermerel. It will be the second driveway on the right.

FERME DE L'HERMEREL
Hosts: Agnes and Francois Lemarie
14230 Géfosse, Fontenay, France
tel: 31.22.64.12
4 Rooms, all w/private bath or shower/WC
Single: 180F, Double: 250F, Triple: 320F
Table d'Hôte: 75F per person
Open all year
No English spoken
Region: Normandy

The Verjus family's historic farm inn is found in a lovely pastoral setting; on a hill, overlooking green pastures and hills. The only sounds disturbing the rural quiet are cow and sheep bells and a variety of lovely birdsongs. The farmhouse is full of historic character, with vaulted ceilings and an old fireplace in the cosy dining room. Built in 1100 and enlarged in the 1700s, the inn combines clean, modern comfort with a traditional ambiance. Home-style dinners usually begin with a regional aperitif called a "macvin", which is a potent combination of white wine and whisky, followed by several courses of delicious dishes made with fresh farm ingredients. Guest bedrooms are newly installed and offer good lighting and spotless private showers and WCs. Fresh light pine furniture and pretty floral print curtains create an appropriately rustic country atmosphere. *Directions:* Geruge is located approximately 10 kilometers south of Lons le Saunier, capital of the Jura department of France. From Lons, follow designated scenic route D117 through the village of Macornay, and continue up the winding road to Geruge, always following signs for the direction of St Julien. Once in Geruge, look for signs directing you to the left for Ferme Auberge La Grange Rouge which is located just outside of the village.

LA GRANGE ROUGE
Hosts: Anne-Marie and Henri Verjus
Geruge, 39570 Lons le Saunier, France
tel: 84.47.00.44
5 Rooms, all with private shower/WC
Single: 150F, Double: 170F, Triple: 220F
Ferme Auberge: 80F per person
Open all year
No English spoken
Region: Jura

Young hosts Isabelle and Pierre Breton run a delightful ferme auberge restaurant with rooms in a lovely setting of rolling hills and pasturelands. Dating from 1770, their large farmhouse of regional grey stone is one of the oldest houses in the Cantal region and is filled with historic ambiance, especially in the guest dining room which has exposed stone walls, a large open-hearthed fireplace and a rarely seen type of stone alcove, originally used as a sink area and preparation kitchen. Country antique furniture and dried flower bouquets complete the rustic scene where guests enjoy delicious, traditional meals featuring farm-fresh meat products. Bedrooms are furnished simply, yet contain charming accents such as brass beds and old armoires. Located in the former attic, the rooms are small and intimate with sloping, beamed ceilings and dormer windows which let in the pure Auvergne air and look out over the unspoilt countryside. *Directions:* Giou de Mamou is located approximately 8 kilometers east of Auillac. Take N122 in the direction of Vic sur Cere and Murat. About 5 kilometers out of Auillac, look for a sign to the left indicating the hamlet of Giou de Mamou via D58. Follow signs indicating Chambres et Tables d'Hôtes Barathe which lead down a country lane to the Bretons' charming establishment.

FERME DE BARATHE
Hosts: Isabelle and Pierre Breton
15130 Giou de Mamou, France
tel: 71.64.61.72
5 Rooms, all with private shower and WC
Demi-pension obligatory: 145F per person
Table d'Hôte: included in lodging rate
Open all year
Some English spoken
Region: Auvergne

For friends or a large family who are looking for an inexpensive abode while exploring Provence, Les Martins makes a very attractive choice. (It would help if one of one of your group understands a little French since the Perons do not speak English.) The main house where the family lives is a typical old mas (farmhouse). The guestrooms are located in an annex located a short stroll up a little lane. Here you will find another characterful building with exposed stone exterior, windows framed with brown shutters and a roof of heavy tile. The four bedrooms share a pleasant lounge area which is attractively decorated by a large antique wooden table surrounded by country-style chairs. Adding to the rustic, country ambiance of the room are some antique farm instruments artfully displayed on the walls. Doors open on to a sunny terrace also shared by all. The bedrooms are basic in door and ambiance, but for the price, certainly adequate. *Directions:* Gordes is located about 38 km east of Avignon. Although the address is Gordes, Les Martins is actually located much closer to the tiny village of Les Beaumettes if you can find it on your map. From the N100, take the 103 north toward Gordes. In about 2km there is a Gîte sign on the left side of the road. Turn left and in a few minutes you will see Les Martins on your left.

LES MARTINS
Hosts: Denise & Claude Peron
84220 Gordes, France
tel: 90.72.24.15
4 Rooms, 3 with private bath/WC
Single: 160F, Double: 190F, Triple: 220F
Table d'Hôte: 70F per person
Credit cards: None
Open February to November 15
No English spoken
Region: Provence

When the Konings family (whose home was Holland) asked a realtor to find a place for them to retire in Provence, they expected the search to take many years. Amazingly, the perfect property, a very old stone farmhouse with great potential charm, was found almost immediately. So, even though the timing was a bit sooner than anticipated, they bought the farmhouse and restored it into an absolute dream.   The six guest rooms are in a cluster of weathered stone buildings which form a small courtyard.   The name of each room gives a clue as to its original use such as "The Old Kitchen", The Hayloft", "The Wine Press", etc.   Arja Konings has exquisite taste and each room is decorated using country antiques and Provençal fabrics.   Most conveniently, the Konings' son, Gerald, (who was born in the United States, is a talented chef.   He oversees the small restaurant which is delightfully appealing with massive beamed ceiling, tiled floor, exposed stone walls and country-style antique furnishings.   The dining room opens onto a terrace which overlooks the swimming pool. *Directions:* Gordes is located about 38 km northeast of Avignon.   From Gordes, head east the D2 for about 2 km.   Turn right (south) on D156.   In just a few minutes you will see La Ferme de la Huppe on your right.

LA FERME DE LA HUPPE
Hosts: Family Konings
Route 156
84220 Gordes, France
tel: 90.72.12.25 fax: 90.72.01.83
6 Rooms, all with private bath/WC
Double: 500F
Gourmet restaurant
Credit cards: MC, VS
Closed January to March 15
Fluent English spoken
Region: Provence

For a tranquil little hideaway while exploring the beautiful area of Provence, the Domaine du Bois Vert is truly a gem. Although only a few years old, the clever owners, Jean Peter and Veronique Richard, have tastefully achieved the ambiance of an old farm house by incorporating a typical pinky tan stuccoed exterior, light blue wooden shutters and a heavy tiled roof. The mood of antiquity continues within where dark beamed ceilings, tiled floors, dark wooden doors, and white walls enhance a few carefully chosen country-style Provençal pieces of furniture. There are only two bedrooms, but each is immaculately tidy and prettily decorated. The bedroom to the back of the house is especially enticing with windows looking out onto the oak trees. By the time you arrive, the proposed swimming pool will probably be completed. Meals are not served on a regular basis, but Veronique treats guests who stay a week to a dinner featuring typical regional specialties. *Directions:* Grans is located approximately 40 km east of Arles and 6 km from Salon de Provence. From Grans, go south for on D19 (signposted to Lançon-Provence). About 1 km after you pass Grans, turn left on a small road where you will see a Gîte sign. In a few minutes turn left again at another Gîte sign and take the lane to the Domaine du Bois Vert.

DOMAINE DU BOIS VERT
Hosts: Veronique & Jean Peter Richard
Quartier Montauban, 13450 Grans, France
tel: 90.55.82.98
2 Rooms, 2 with private bath/WC
Single: 190-230F, Double: 210-250F, Triple 310-350F
No Table d'Hôte
Credit cards: None
Open all year
Good English spoken
Region: Provence

The Paulous are a friendly, well-travelled couple who have filled their 300-year-old cottage with antiques and artifacts from their many voyages. A low, stone doorway leads into the main room of their house which they have transformed into a very cosy dining room/kitchen area. This welcoming room has a low, beamed ceiling, stone walls, walk-in fireplace and country antique furniture and is an inviting spot to linger with Monsieur and Madame over breakfast which, on warm mornings, is enjoyed with good conversation on the sunny courtyard terrace. Madame Paulou is also happy to bring breakfast to the room on a tray. The Paulous offer a charming, twin-bedded guest room which has an entrance completely independent of the rest of the house. Furnishings are tasteful, clean and fresh, accented by an interesting carved chest and artwork from their son's travels in Korea. This is a real jewel of a bed and breakfast, made even more delightful by the warm welcome extended by the Paulous. *Directions:* Loyan, referenced by the larger, neighboring town of Guidel, is located approximately 10 kilometers east of Lorient or 58 kilometers southeast of Quimper. Leave Guidel on D162 in the direction of Ploemeur. This country road has many twists and turns, so be sure to continue following signs to Ploemeur. Just after passing the sign at the entry of the tiny hamlet of Loyan, turn into the first driveway on the left.

CHEZ PAULOU
Hosts: Monsieur and Madame Paulou
Route de Ploemeur, Loyan, 56520 Guidel, France
tel: 97.86.34.85
1 Room, with private shower/WC
Single: 170F, Double: 180F, Triple: 250F
No Table d'Hôte
Open all year
Very little English spoken
Region: Brittany

A romantic, enchanted quality pervades the lovely old Moulin de la Dive, a former flour mill covered with ivy and surrounded by magical wooded grounds. Originally built by a noble family in the 14th century, the mill was burned by the Protestants in 1569 and rebuilt in the early 17th century, only to be burned again during the French Revolution. Annick Vanverts and her husband are extremely warm and solicitous hosts who relocated here from Paris, seeking a more natural existence away from the fast pace and pollution of the big city. Guests have a private entrance through an old arched doorway and up a marble staircase to the two upstairs bedrooms, each uniquely decorated. Seville is furnished entirely in Spanish antiques, and Nohant reflects the graceful style of 18th-century France and is named after the home of French novelist Georges Sand. All the rooms have spotless, modern bathrooms and large windows which let in the pure country air. Breakfast is enjoyed either in the Vanverts' charming, country-elegant salon or outside in the lush garden. *Directions:* Guron is located approximately 30 kilometers southwest of Poitiers. Take N10 in the direction of Angouleme for about 25 kilometers past the village of Les Minieres, then turn left onto D29 towards the town of Auche. Two kilometers later look for a Chambres d'Hôtes sign marking the Vanverts' gate on the right.

LE MOULIN DE LA DIVE
Hosts: Monsieur and Madame Vanverts
Guron, 86700 Payre, France
tel: 49.42.40.97
2 Rooms, both with private WC/bath or shower
Single: 290-310F, Double: 330-350F, Triple: 430F
No Table d'Hôte
Open July and August
Very little English spoken
Region: Atlantic Coast

A stay at Chez Boch is like a visit to an aunt in the country, offering a chance to relax in a home-like atmosphere, looked after by solicitous hostess Frieda Boch. Her contemporary chalet-style house is found in a suburb of Heiligenstein and is furnished with an assortment of knicknacks, prints and souvenirs that form an eclectic collection of memorabilia. Bedrooms are comfortable and somewhat basic, furnished in a mix of antique and reproduction furniture. An adjoining annex has a sitting room with a television, refrigerator and sink for guests' use. Breakfast is also served here on a cheerful enclosed porch, bordered by bright red geranium plants. Frieda serves a particularly delicious and substantial morning buffet consisting of a large selection of coffee cakes and breads, several varieties of cheeses and cold cuts, four kinds of preserves, honey and the usual choice of hot coffee, tea or chocolate. *Directions:* Heiligenstein is located approximately 28 kilometers southwest of Strasbourg. Take N422 past the turnoff to Obernai and just before the town of Barr look for the turnoff to Heiligenstein to the right. Once in Heiligenstein, go through town following the directions for Obernai. The Boch house is on the left on the road out of town and is marked with a Chambres d'Hôtes sign.

CHEZ BOCH
Hostess: Madame Frieda Boch
144, rue Principale
67140 Heiligenstein, France
tel: 88.08.97.30
4 Rooms, all with pvt WC/bath or shower
Single: 150F, Double: 180-200F, Triple: 240-250F
No Table d'Hôte
Open all year
No English spoken, fluent German spoken
Region: Alsace

The Jehls are a farming family who have been offering guest accommodation in their comfortable home for the past eight years. Madame Jehl and her daughter Clarisse cheerfully attend to all aspects of their bed and breakfast, making sure that all guests feel right at home. Bedrooms are modest yet comfortable, each with private shower, wash basin, and WC. All are basic, yet very clean and pleasant, furnished with reproduction furniture and decorated in earth tones. Four of the rooms have French doors which open onto a balcony bordered with pots of bright red geraniums. The courtyard/parking lot below is a popular gathering place where guests enjoy drinks and conversation before dinner. Meals are enjoyed together at one long table and feature generous portions of home-cooked regional dishes. For a culinary change of pace, the renowned L'Auberge de L'Ill is a highly rated gourmet restaurant located nearby at the edge of the village on the banks of the tranquil Ill River. *Directions:* Illhaeusern is located approximately 20 kilometers north of Colmar. Take N83 north towards Selestat and Strasbourg. After about 15 kilometers, turn right onto D106 to Guemar and Illhaeusern. Once in the village, just past the church, look for a Chambres d'Hôtes sign which marks the Jehls' driveway on the left.

MAISON D'HÔTE JEHL
Hostess: Madame Jehl
33, rue du 25 Janvier
68150 Illhaeusern, France
tel: 89.71.83.76
6 Rooms, all w/private WC/shower
Single: 190F, Double: 190-230F, Triple: 330F
Table d'Hôte: 185F
Open all year except month of February
Some English spoken, also fluent German
Region: Alsace

The old manor house of Le Petit Pey is set in pretty grounds and tended with care by energetic hostess Annie de Bosredon, a very charming, refined, yet down-to-earth hostess who takes great pleasure in opening her home to guests. Le Petit Pey is a regional stone building with windows and French doors framed by white shutters. The oldest part dates from the 1600s, while the "newer" wing was added in about 1760. Madame de Bosredon's aristocratic drawing room combines comfort and elegance and is filled with valuable antiques, artifacts and fresh-cut garden roses. Bedrooms are furnished in family antiques, and each has its own country charm. The drawing room and bedrooms actually are in a separate wing of the house, so guests are afforded privacy and the luxury of being at home in the lovely salon. There are plenty of historic walled towns in the region as well as the interesting towns of Issigeac and Bergerac. *Directions:* Issigeac is approximately 60 kilometers south of Périgueux via 21 through Bergerac. About 11 kilometers after Bergerac, turn left onto D14 towards Issigeac, then at Issigeac take D21 towards Castillonnes. Two kilometers later at Monmarves, look for a sign reading Domaine du Petit Pey and turn into the green gate.

LE PETIT PEY
Hostess: Madame Annie de Bosredon
Service de Réservation Loisirs et Accueil
16, rue Wilson, 24000 Périgeux, France
Tel. 53.53.99.99 or 53.58.70.61
2 Rooms, both w/pvt WC and shower
Single: 280F, Double: 310F
No Table d'Hôte
Open all year
Good English spoken
Region: Périgord

Bed & Breakfast Descriptions

The Chateau du Plessis is a lovely, aristocratic country home, truly one of France's most exceptional private chateaux-hotels and a personal favorite; one of the few establishments that we are including in both our guidebooks to France. Madame Benoist's family have lived here since well before the revolution, but the antiques throughout the home are later acquisitions of her great, great, great grandfather, as the furnishings original to the house were burned on the front lawn by the revolutionaries in 1793. Furnishings throughout the home are elegant, yet the Benoists also establish an atmosphere of homey comfort. Artistic fresh flower arrangements abound and one can see Madame's cutting garden from the French doors in the salon that open onto the lush grounds. In the evening the large oval table in the dining room provides an opportunity to enjoy the company of other guests and the country-fresh cuisine of Madame Benoist. The Benoists are a handsome couple who take great pride in their home and the welcome they extend to their guests. *Directions:* To reach La Jaille-Yvon travel north of Angers on N162 and at the town of Le Lion d'Angers clock the odometer eleven kilometers further north to an intersection, Carrefour Fleur de Lys. Turn east and travel 2 1/2 kilometers to La Jaille-Yvon - the Château du Plessis on its southern edge.

CHÂTEAU DU PLESSIS
Hosts: Monsiuer and Madame Paul Benoist
49990 La Jaille-Yvon
tel: 41.95.12.75   fax: 41.95.14.41
8 Rooms, all w/pvt baths
Double: 580-730F
Table d'Hôte: 250F per person
Open March 1 to November 1
Credit cards: All major
Good English spoken
Region: West Loire Valley

Young Jacques and Valerie Advenier are charming hosts who are dedicated to the restoration of Jacques' family chateau and to preserving a peaceful and refined ambiance. Their enchanting home is found in an area rich in history; the region of France which was once home to the ruling Bourbon family. A fascinating collection of ancient fortresses and castles can be visited throughout the surrounding countryside. During the day, Jacques and Valerie open their gracious oak-panelled dining room to the public and offer tea, coffee and homemade pastries. The lovely room is set with round tables covered with pretty floral print tablecloths and is also where guests enjoy leisurely breakfasts and candlelit dinners. A beautiful wide stone stairway leads upstairs to the inviting guest bedrooms, all of which Jacques has lovingly restored and decorated with impeccable taste and attention to detail, including direct dial phones in each room. Furnished in fine antiques, lovely fabrics, rugs and artwork, each room is a delightful haven for travellers. *Directions:* Jaligny is located approximately 40 kilometers north of Vichy. Travel via D906 or N209 to D907 to Lapalisse then leave town on D480 to Jaligny, Dompierre. Go through the town of Jaligny, leaving on D989 towards the town of le Donjon. Not quite 2 kilometers out of town, look for a sign to the right for Le Lonzat. A lovely tree-lined drive curves around to the entrance.

CHATEAU DE LONZAT
Hosts: Jacques and Valerie Advenier
03220 Jaligny sur Besbre, France
tel: 70.34.73.39 fax: 70.34.81.31
5 Rooms, all w/private WC/bath
Single: 306-606F, Double: 352-692F, Triple: 608-808F
Table d'Hôte: 130F per person
Open March 1 through December 31
Some English spoken
Region: Berry

The Chaffois cottage is found in a beautiful mountain setting where grassy hillsides are broken only by delicate wildflowers and grazing horses. Bernard and Mireille Chaffois are an attractive, friendly couple who, in addition to offering bed and breakfast accommodation also grow lavender to make perfume and raise goats to produce fresh homemade goat cheese. Their charming home dates from 1600 and is simply, yet comfortably furnished. Guest bedrooms are located upstairs and have an independent guest entrance and a spacious sitting area. In the mornings guests wake to fresh country bread and plenty of hot *cafe au lait* served in large pottery pitchers. This traditional French country fare is served in the historical dining room which features vaulted stone ceilings. *Directions:* Jansac is located approximately 60 kilometers southeast of Valence. If arriving via autoroute from Lyon, exit at Valence Sud (south exit of Valence) and follow directions for Crest on D111. Continue past the large town of Die about 15 kilometers to the village of Récoubeau. Go through town and then turn right following signs for Jansac: the road winds up into the mountains to this tiny hamlet. The Chaffois' home is impossible to miss because part of the house forms an arch over the road and is marked with a sign.

CHEZ CHAFFOIS
Hosts: Bernard and Mireille Chaffois
Récoubeau-Jansac, 26310, France
tel: 75.21.30.46
3 Rooms, 1 w/pvt shower/others share
Single: 150F, Double: 180F, Triple: 220F
Table d'Hôte: 70F
Open all year
Very little English spoken
Region: Alps

Twelve years ago Christel Hofstadt came on holiday from Germany and fell in love with the absolute tranquility surrounding the Mas Soupetrière. Although the stone farm building was in complete disrepair, she could not resist buying it. The house has been completely renovated and is open as a delightful bed and breakfast. The facade of the house is very attractive: a combination of honey-colored stone interspersed with light tan stuccoed walls, heavy tiled roof and light gray-blue shutters. Christel has excellent taste and the decor is fresh and pretty: country antiques, provençal-style fabrics, white plastered walls, and oriental carpets. Meals are usually served outside on a pretty terrace in front of the house (a hearty dinner, featuring the specialties of Provence and wine, is included in the room rate). An added bonus is the swimming pool located in a field near the house. Apartments are also available, but we prefer the main house. *Directions:* Gordes is located 38 km northeast of Avignon. From N100, take D60 north toward Joucas. Before Joucas, turn right (east) on the D2. Turn left at the first road (marked 102) and take the very first lane to your right. In a few minutes you will see the bed and breakfast on your left.

MAS DE LA SOUPETRIÈRE
Host: Mme Christel Hofstadt
Joucas
84220 Gordes, France
tel: 90.05.78.81 fax: 90.05.76.33
3 Rooms, all with private bath/WC
Half Pension Basis:
Single: 620F, Double: 760F
Table d'Hôte included in room rate
Open all year
Fluent English spoken
Region: Provence

A winding country road leads to the Renevots' modest farmhouse in this typically Breton region of farmlands dotted with white stone houses. The Renevots raise dairy cows and poultry on their farm which has been in Monsieur's family for several generations. The original stone farmhouse has been transformed into a comfortable apartment for stays of a week or more. Next door, the Renevots now live in a newer house where they offer an upstairs and downstairs bedroom to bed and breakfast guests. Decor is simple and home-like and bedrooms are small. The house does not have an historic ambiance, but the welcome provided by Madame Rénévot is very warm and sincere. She enjoys opening her parlour to guests and is happy to give advice on planning sightseeing tours in the area. The scenic Brittany coast is only minutes away, as is the picturesque town of Quimper. If you seek a true "slice" of French country farm life, a stay at the Rénévots' will not disappoint. *Directions:* Le Juch is located approximately 20 kilometers northwest of Quimper. Take D765 towards Douarnenez then after approximately 16 kilometers look for a sign to the right for Le Juch. Just after entering the village, you will see a cemetery on the left: take the next right in the direction of Guengat, then turn at the second right which is marked Route Tar-ar and leads to the Rénévots' white cottage.

KERSANTEC
Hosts: Yvette and René Rénévot
29100 Le Juch, France
tel: 98.74.71.36
2 Rooms, both with private bath, share WC
Single: 150F, Double: 180F
No Table d'Hôte
Open all year
No English spoken
Region: Brittany

Madame and Monsieur Chatel, and their two sons, aged two and seven, delight in welcoming guests into their pretty Norman farmhouse. The Chatels restored this 200-year-old farmhouse over a period of several years and now have a comfortable, independent wing for their guests. A Dutch door leads to the downstairs foyer where the Chatels have placed a wealth of local sightseeing and restaurant information on an antique table. The three bedrooms are all fresh and clean, with the downstairs room being particularly charming as it contains an antique bed and armoire. Morning baguettes are enjoyed outdoors on the guest terrace or in the delightful living/dining room with its beamed ceilings, pretty antique furniture and a collection of old plates. The original "walk-in" stone fireplace provides a cosy blaze on cool mornings and evenings. The Chatels have been welcoming bed and breakfast guests since 1983 and are solicitous hosts, always ready with advice on the many local sights and excursions. *Directions:* Jumièges is located approximately 23 kilometers east of Rouen via D982, then D143. In Jumièges look for a green and yellow Chambres d'Hôtes sign directing you to leave town on a small country road and continue for about 1 kilometer to the Chatels' low, stone farmhouse with a Gîtes de France sign outside.

CHEZ CHATEL
Hosts: Monsieur and Madame Chatel
Rue de Quesney
76480 Jumièges, France
tel: 35.37.24.98
3 Rooms, all with sink/WC, 2 share shower
Single: 150F, Double: 180F
No Table d'Hôte
Open all year
No English spoken
Region: Normandy

It is tempting not to "share" the discovery of the Mas du Bas Claux - it is just too perfect.   Judy (who is English) and Jan (who is Dutch) bought this beautiful piece of property (located just outside the charming medieval village of Lacoste) when Jan took early retirement from the DuPont Company.   It took several years of dedicated labor, but what had been a neglected 18th-century stone farmhouse is now a beautiful home. Jan is a keen gardener and, when the house was redesigned, the setting was also restructured so that what had been a sloping field is now a dramatic, beautifully-manicured, grassy terrace with a romantic outlook over the vineyards and beyond to the beckoning hills.   Also in the garden there is a delightful swimming pool, a lovely place to relax after a day of sightseeing.   It is not the beauty of the house or garden, however, which make this place so perfect: it is the warmth of the owners, Judy and Jan, who are perfect hosts.   They are not listed in any of the "official" bed and breakfast organizations because they wish to remain small and exclusive, maintaining the size and quality to treat each and everyone as a friend and pampered guest.   *Directions:* Lacoste is located 45 km east of Avignon.   Take the D108 east from Lacoste.   After 1 km, watch for a sign on the left side of the road for Mas du Bas Claux.

MAS DU BAS CLAUX
Hosts: Judy & Jan van Horck
84480 Lacoste, France
tel:90.75.90.49
2 Rooms, both with private bath/WC
Single: 350F, Double: 400F, Triple: 450F
No Table d'Hote
Credit cards: None
Open all year
Fluent English spoken
Region: Provence

In the heart of a picturesque hill town at the foot of a castle once home to the infamous Marquis de Sade, Monsieur Court de Gebelin offers exquisite accommodation in his charming 17th-century home. Monsieur has spent several years lovingly restoring and improving his house to achieve a harmonious mix of historic surroundings with the latest in modern conveniences. Bedrooms are furnished in understated good taste and feature subdued lighting and luxurious private baths. Each room is unique in its design and decor, with the high level of comfort and attention to detail remaining uniform throughout. As an added luxury for guests, Monsieur has installed a small, jewel-like swimming pool beside the upstairs terrace where guests are invited to relax after a day of sightseeing, or simply to escape summer's midday heat. The sincere, warm welcome offered by Monsieur Court de Gebelin and his mother complete the perfection of the unforgettable Relais du Procureur. *Directions:* From Avignon take N100 towards Apt, turning right at the village of Lumières following signs for Lacoste. Once in the village, the route to the Relais du Procureur is well marked, although the narrow old streets can be difficult to navigate in a large car.

RELAIS DU PROCUREUR
Host: Antoine Court de Gebelin
Rue Basse
84710 Lacoste, France
tel: 90.75.82.28 fax: 90.75.86.94
Book by phone only, major credit cards OK
6 Rooms, all with private bath/WC
Single: 410F, Double: 410-460F, Triple: 500F
No Table d'Hôte
Open all year
Very good English spoken
Region: Provence

Monsieur and Madame Rebiffe take great pleasure in welcoming bed and breakfast guests into their 300-year-old farmhouse. The house is characteristically long and low, built of pretty, regional stone and situated in a scenic region where Monsieur Rebiffe enjoys guiding horse drawn carriage trips. Madame is fond of cooking regional Table d'Hôte dinners including specialties such as pork with wild mushroom or chestnut sauces, garlic soup and black cherry cobbler. She lived in Washington and New York in the mid-1940s and retains a fair fluency in English through her love of literature. Guest have a private entrance into a cosy sitting room with exposed stone walls, old fireplace, comfy couch, easy chairs and a bookcase full of English and French classics. Upstairs, the bedrooms have pretty views over the surrounding countryside and are comfortably furnished with a mixture of family furniture. *Directions:* Ladignac le Long is located approximately 35 kilometers south of Limoges. Take D704 towards St Yriex la Perche, turning right about 5 kilometers after the village of St Maurice les Brosses onto D15 to Nexon. Before the castle at the entrance to Nexon, turn left to Ladignac le Long. Go through Ladignac and follow signs for the hamlet of Mazerollas. In 4 km, at the little intersection of Mazerollas, turn left towards Bourdoulet. The Rebiffe farm is 300 metres on the right marked with a Chambres d'Hôtes sign.

CHEZ REBIFFE
Hosts: Monsieur and Madame Rebiffe
Mazerollas, 87500 Ladignac le Long, France
tel: 55.09.35.92
2 Rooms share one bath/WC
Single: 115F, Double: 135F, Triple: 190F
Table d'Hôte: 65F per person
Open all year
Good English spoken by Madame Rebiffe
*   Périgord*

Bed & Breakfast Descriptions

Martine and Jean-Pierre Halope and their two young daughters live in their restored farmhouse in a tranquil countryside setting. The neat and tidy buildings are of light-coloured regional stone and have a storybook farm feeling. Farm animals abound, as the Halopes raise horses, cows, chickens, geese, goats and dogs. Guests may sample farm produce and livestock at the family Table d'Hôte dinners served at a long wooden table in the breakfast/dining room. An old stone fireplace warms the room on cool mornings and evenings. The Halopes' homey living room is also open to guests and is a pleasant spot to enjoy an aperitif or afternoon tea. The simple, yet charming guest bedrooms are offer peaceful views of the surrounding fields and nearby woods. All is fresh and newly renovated in the rooms, each decorated in a different pastel color scheme. Perfectly located for touring the castles of the Loire Valley, the Ferme de l'Épeigne offers comfortable bed and breakfast accommodation in a busy family home. *Directions:* Langeais is located approximately 22 kilometers west of Tours on the north bank of the Loire. Take N152 to Langeais, then follow signs for the town of Hommes via D15. After 2 kilometers there is a Chambres d'Hôtes sign on the right indicating L'Épeigne.

LA FERME DE L'ÉPEIGNE
Hosts: Martine and Jean-Pierre Halope
37130 Langeais, France
tel: 47.96.54.23 or 47.96.37.13
5 Rooms, 3 w/pvt WC/shower, rest share
Single: 180-200F, Double: 210-250F, Triple: 260-300F
Table d'Hôte 90-100F per person
  (advance notice requested)
Open all year
No English spoken
Region: Loire Valley

A tree-shaded drive leads up to the Chateau de Larçay built in 1830 at the height of the "romantic" period of French history. A happy collie dog peeking out from behind bright red garden tomatoes lined up on the kitchen window ledge welcomed us to this small castle.   Inside, the friendly Le Sage family has taken great pleasure and pride in retaining the original flavour of the castle while adding modern conveniences.   Bedrooms are all unique and carefully decorated by Madame Le Sage in authentic furniture and fabrics reflecting the different styles of the romantic era. Madame is rightfully proud of the exquisite Louis XVI suite furnished in period antiques, old Bordeaux silk bedspreads and complementing wallpaper.   The downstairs salon has been preserved in its original state, boasting wood panelling which also dates from the time of Louis XVI.   Be sure to allow time to enjoy Madame Le Sage's breakfast of croissants and preserves served on the front terrace, as there is no more peaceful place to begin the day than here, watching the sunlight slanting through the trees and listening to lilting birdsongs. *Directions:*   Larcay is located 6 kilometers east of Tours on the south bank of the Loire.   Take N76 in the direction of Vierzon to Larçay where you turn right at the traffic light opposite the church.   The road climbs a short distance to the chateau's gate on the right.

CHATEAU DE LARÇAY
Hosts: André and Collette Le Sage
37270 Larçay, France
tel: 47.50.39.39
3 Rooms/2 Suites, all with pvt WC/bath or shower
Single: 250-300F, Double: 450-700F, Triple: 600+F
No Table d'Hôte
Open all year
Very good English spoken
Region: Loire Valley

The seaside town of Larmor Plage is a popular summer destination for sailors, windsurfers and sightseers. For travellers seeking this type of beachtown ambiance, the Allanos offer very comfortable and clean accommodation in their suburban home. The front entry hall sets the tone of this genteel home with old pictures, antiques and fresh flower arrangements. A faux marble staircase leads upstairs to guest rooms which are comfortably furnished in antique reproductions. The downstairs guest bedroom has an independent French door entry which leads to a flagstone terrace and the Allanos' tranquil lawn and garden. Furnished in family antiques, this is a pretty, though somewhat small, room. A possible drawback is the house's proximity to the often heavily trafficked road, yet the Allanos have a faithful returning clientele who enjoy their oasis of comfort in this summer resort community. *Directions:* Larmor Plage is located 5 kilometers south of L'Orient. Once in Larmor Plage, go through town and follow the route for Kerpape which will turn into the beachfront road rue des Roseaux. Look for a small Chambres d'Hôtes sign on the gatepost of number 9 which will be on the left. The Allanos' white house is not easily visible from the road.

VILLA LES CAMELIAS
Hosts: Monsieur and Madame Allano
9, rue des Roseaux
56260 Larmor Plage, France
tel: 97.65.50.67
4 Rooms, all w/private bath or shower and WC
Single: 180F, Double: 200F
No Table d'Hôte
Open all year
Very little English spoken
Region: Brittany

A narrow cobblestone alley leads to the entrance of La Taverne de la Dame du Plô, a convivial piano bar and gathering place in a brick and half-timbered house dating from the Middle Ages and full of historical flavour. Bernard Fevre and his father are the talented team who have artfully and lovingly restored their medieval house into a cellar piano bar and bed and breakfast. A separate entrance leads to the charming guest accommodation; small, intimate rooms tastefully decorated with dainty print wallpapers in soft color tones, furnished with choice country antique pieces. All have a tiny private shower and basin area and private WC. Breakfast can be enjoyed in the garden across the lane or in the adjoining dining room. There is also a small kitchen area for guests' use. *Directions:* Lavaur is located approximately 30 km east of Toulouse. Take D112 and enter the town of Lavaur, following signs for centre ville (the town centre). At the roundabout with the fountain, take La Grande Rue (the main street) and follow it to the old part of town where it will narrow and its name will change to rue Père Colin. After the road veers to the right, look for a Chambres d'Hôtes sign on the right marking the Fevres' three-story brick house on a corner. The cross street is rue Carlipa.

LA TAVERNE DE LA DAME DU PLÔ
Host: Monsieur Bernard Fevre
5, rue Père Colin
81500 Lavaur, France
tel: 63.41.38.77
4 Rooms, all w/pvt WC/shower
Single: 170F, Double: 200F, Triple: 230F
No Table d'Hôte
Open all year
Good English spoken
Region: Tarn

If you want to experience a stay in a typical French farmhouse, Montpeyroux (a handsome large two-story home, softened by ivy and white shutters) makes an excellent choice.   The ambiance within does not conform to any trendy decorating scheme - this is truly a family home with old-fashioned furnishings.   Yet, I was quite impressed: the bedrooms are all wall papered and have color coordinated draperies, cushions, and bedspreads - all beautifully sewn by Mme Sallier.   Splurge and request the most expensive room - not just because it is the largest and the only one with a private bathroom, but because it also is just beautiful with genuine antiques set off by a color scheme of creams and greens.   The farm also has its own swimming pool and tennis court - quite a surprise for such a simple farmhouse. *Directions:* Castres is located 71km east of Toulouse.   From Castres go southwest on N126 then D622 toward Revel.   About 18km after leaving Castres turn north on D12 to Lempaut.   From Lempaut drive west on D46 for about 2km.   When you come to a large cemetery on your left, turn left on the small road just before the cemetery.   The road loops around the cemetery.   Follow this road until you see the Gîte sign and the large house on your right.

MONTPEYROUX
Hosts: M & Mme A. Sallier
Montpeyroux, Lempaut
81700 Puylaurens, France
tel: 63.75.51.17
5 Rooms, 1 with private bath/WC
Single: 200F, Double: 250-300F
Table d'Hôte: 80 F per person
Credit cards: None
Open April to November
No English spoken
Region: Tarn

Cécile and Jan Balsem are energetic hosts who have renovated their 250-year-old farmhouse into a simple, yet very atmospheric home. Jan is originally from Holland and speaks fluent French, English, German and, of course, Dutch. In his spare time he is a hang-gliding enthusiast, and willingly escorts guests on sojourns in the local countryside. His warm, friendly wife Cécile is a talented watercolourist who also finds time to make homemade breads and preserves plus look after their children, an extensive vegetable garden and assorted farm animals. Bedrooms are high-ceilinged and spacious, furnished in family antiques and decorated with dainty wallpapers and fresh flower bouquets. The atmosphere Chez Balsem is relaxed and no-frills; with renovation still in progress, but rough edges removed, it is easy to be captivated by the Balsems' open-hearted welcome and lovely hilltop location. *Directions:* Lhopital is located about 40 kilometers southwest of Geneva. Take autoroute A40 to the Bellegarde exit, number 10. Follow signs for Seyssel. Continue about 10 kilometers to the village of Lhopital and look for a Chambres d'Hôtes sign that directs to the left up a steep, narrow road. The Balsems' stone house is on the left at the top of the road.

CHEZ BALSEM
Hosts: Jan and Cécile Balsem
01420 Lhopital, France
tel: 50.59.50.58
3 Rooms, share 1 bath/WC
Single: 100F, Double: 140F, Triple: 180F
Table d'Hôte: 60F per person
Open all year
Very good English spoken
Region: Rhône/Alps

Bed and breakfast at the Domaine de Gradille means home-like, family accommodation in a countryside setting full of bucolic charm. A pretty footpath leads to a nearby lake, completely hidden by lush deciduous woods, where guests may swim in the refreshing water. Warm and friendly hosts Monsieur and Madame Soulié offer three guest rooms in their family farmhouse and two modern bedrooms, each with private bath and WC, in a recently remodeled adjoining building. Bedrooms exhibit a mixture of decor and taste, but are very comfortable and have personal touches such as bud vases of fresh flowers. Two of the rooms have lovely views over tranquil pastures and hills. Guests usually gather in the early evening on the terrace or in the tiny bar for a delicious sample of the Soulies' homemade fruit liqueurs. Table d'Hôte dinners are served "en famille" in the cosy dining room and feature several courses of carefully prepared dishes. *Directions:* Domaine de Gradille is located about 14 kilometers past Lisle sur Tarn, a total of approximately 50 kilometers northeast of Toulouse. Take N88 in the direction of Albi, turning left at Gaillac onto D999 in the direction of Montauban, then 4 kilometers outside of Gaillac, look for Chambres d'Hôtes signs directing you to a small road on the right. Take the first driveway on the right to the Souliés' white, two-storey tile- roofed farmhouse.

DOMAINE DE GRADILLE
Hosts: Monsieur and Madame Soulié
81310 Lisle sur Tarn, France
tel: 63.41.01.57
5 Rooms, all with private bath or shower, 3 share WC
Single: 125-160F, Double: 145-180F, Triple: 205-250F
Table d'Hôte: 70F per person
Open all year
Good English spoken, also Spanish
Region: Tarn

The Chaumière de Kerisac is one of our most picturesque bed and breakfasts, offering comfortable accommodation in a lovely, country setting, complemented by cultivated hosts. The Cheilletz-Maignans' charming, thatch-roofed house has been in their family for many years, although it is only since Monsieur's retirement that they returned here on a full-time basis after their many years of living overseas in Morocco and Indochina. Breakfast is served in their cosy salon/dining room filled with family antiques and artifacts from their extensive travels. Low, beamed ceilings and an old stone fireplace enhance the evocative decor. Monsieur and Madame have many fascinating stories to share as does their talented daughter who is a bookbinder by trade. A small exterior stone stairway leads up to two of the guest bedrooms in this long, low stone house, while the third is completely independent and even has a small private garden. Rooms are pleasingly furnished in a mix of antique furniture and pretty floral wallpapers. Madame's attention to detail is evident in her thoughtful touches such as aspirin in the bathrooms and fresh flowers in every room. *Directions:* Locqueltas is about 10 kilometers north of Vannes via D767 then north on D767a to Locqueltas. From here, the way is well marked by Chambres d'Hôtes signs.

CHAUMIÈRE DE KERISAC
Hosts: Monsieur and Madame Cheilletz-Maignan
Locqueltas, D767 - 56390 Grandchamp, France
tel: 97.66.60.13 fax: 97.66.66.73
3 Rooms, all with private bath/2 share WC
Single: 200F, Double: 280F, Triple: 330F
No Table d'Hôte
Open all year
Good English spoken (mainly by daughter)
Region: Brittany

A stay at the lovely Chateau de Longecourt is a wonderful opportunity to experience life in a French country castle.   Surrounded on all sides by a tranquil moat, the castle has a delicate fairy-tale quality enhanced by its graceful towers and neo-classical Italian decoration.   Inside, the elegant, gilt-trimmed salon, dining room, reception rooms and library are all furnished and decorated in authentic antiques from the Louis XV period.   Bedrooms are also highly charming; generously furnished with beautiful antiques, Oriental rugs, paintings and objets d'art.   Each room is unique, with intimate tower bedrooms featuring stone vaulted ceilings and others offering marble fireplaces and tall windows overlooking the peaceful grounds.   The Chateau de Longecourt is as memorable for its exquisite surroundings as for the warm welcome extended by the Comtesse de Saint-Seine and her personable sons.   They make an effort to pamper their guests with luxurious details such as bedtime chocolates and copious breakfasts served on heirloom china.   *Directions:* Longecourt en Plaine is located approximately 15 kilometers southeast of Dijon, on the Burgundy canal.   Leave Dijon on D968 following signs for Longecourt en Plaine.   Once in the village, signs for Chateau de Longecourt point the way to the castle which is located near the church.

* CHATEAU DE LONGECOURT
Hosts: Comtesse Bertrand de Saint-Seine
2, rue du Chateau
Longecourt en Plaine, 21110 Genlis, France
tel: 80.39.88.76
4 Rooms, all w/private WC/bath
Double: 650F
Table d'Hôte: 250F
Open all year
Very little English spoken
Region: Burgundy

Every summer the Belières leave Paris and relocate to their family castle near Loubressac. The chateau dates from 1630 and is highly charming, filled with an assortment of country antiques and artifacts. The Belières have kept the building in more or less its original state, so a very authentic feeling of the past remains, including a musty odour of days gone by. Guests climb up a circular tower staircase to reach the second floor which is devoted entirely to bed and breakfast accommodation. All of the bedrooms are loaded with old fashioned, albeit faded, charm, decorated with old paintings, dainty, flower-print wallpapers, brass or antique beds and dried flower arrangements. There are also apartment-style accommodations available for longer stays which are found in a very quaint adjoining stone building. A casual feeling of a holiday in the country tempts guests to spend entire afternoons relaxing in the walled garden or near the pool, soaking up the tranquil atmosphere. *Directions:* Loubressac is located approximately 45 kilometers northwest of Figeac. Take N140 towards Rocamadour, turning right at Le Bourg towards St Cere. Leave St Cere on D30 in the direction of Carennac and, after a small, old water tower on the right, look for a small sign, also on the right, which says Gramot with an arrow directing to a driveway on the left.

CHATEAU DE GAMOT
Hosts: Monsieur and Madame Belières
46130 Loubressac, France
tel: 65.38.58.50 or 65.38.52.05
or in Paris (1) 48.83.01.91
7 Rooms, 3 w/pvt WC/bath, others share
Single: 180-275F, Double: 250-350F, Triple: 330-400F
No Table d'Hôte
Open all year
Some English spoken
Region: Dordogne/Lot

Michel Descorps resides in a long, low country house reminiscent of stable buildings. He did indeed once keep a full stable of horses here and is a former champion of the French four-in-hand competition. Inside, his ivy-covered "ranch style" home has a very British "country cottage" feeling: in fact, Monsieur avows himself to be quite an Anglophile. Laura Ashley wallpapers such as the pretty, yet understated, "Scottish thistle" pattern decorate the walls in his guest bedrooms, while Cecil Aldin prints brighten the hallways. Bathrooms are all newly renovated and extremely clean, modern and well-equipped. All the accommodation is fresh and very tasteful, with rustic antique furniture and old exposed support beams adding historic character to the rooms. Table d'Hôte dinners are available with advance notice and are served in the cosy dining room full of Cecil Aldin prints on a background of green striped wallpaper. In the morning, guests are pampered with breakfast in their rooms, on the garden terrace or in the dining room. *Directions:* Luynes is located approximately 10 kilometers west of Tours on the north bank of the Loire. Take N152 to Luynes, then turn onto D49 towards Pernay. Continue towards Pernay on D6 and at Le Maupas take the first right turn, after which the first driveway on the right is signposted Le Quart.

LE QUART
Host: Monsieur Michel Descorps
37230 Luynes, France
tel: 47.55.51.70 or 47.48.37.13
4 Rooms, all with private bath
Double: 450-850F
Table d'Hôte: price varies
Open all year
Fluent English spoken
Region: Loire Valley

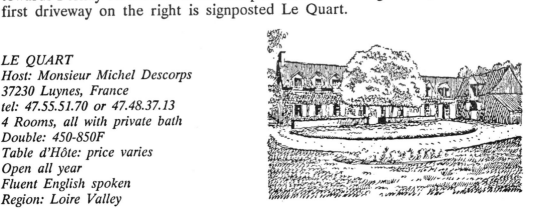

The Marcs are friendly country folk in their 40s who have lived in their ivy-covered former stablehouse for 20 years, while converting it, bit by bit, to the comfortable, if modest home it is today. This is a working farm, where the Marcs raise cattle, sheep, chickens and the occasional goose. Their home is very clean and well-kept: they offer three guest rooms in the main house and an apartment located just across the pretty courtyard. The bedrooms are furnished simply but with taste - antique-style pieces decorate every room, all of which have private bath. The Marcs have made every effort to make their home comfortable and welcoming for guests and are ready to help in any way. Although the Marcs do not speak English, they overcome any language barriers with their warm welcome and farm-style hospitality. *Directions:* Mainneville is located about 75 kilometers northwest of Paris via A15 to Pontoise, then D915 through Gisors, and finally on D14 to Mainneville. In Mainneville, look for a green and yellow Chambres d'Hôtes sign directing you to the Marcs' farm. Located just on the edge of town, the low, ivy-covered house is set back from the road with a lush green lawn and big trees in front. Pretty natural wood shutters flank all the doors and windows.

FERME DE SAINTE GENEVIÈVE
Hosts: Jeannine and Jean-Claude Marc
27150 Mainneville, France
tel: 32.55.51.26
4 Rooms, all with private bath/WC
Single: 160F, Double: 190F, Triple: 260F
No Table d'Hôte
Open all year
Very little English spoken
Region: Normandy

The Derepas' bed and breakfast, set in an imposing stone farmhouse, once the dependent farm of the manor house on the hill above, is recommended for travellers seeking a quiet, countryside setting. Francoise Derepas offers freshly remodelled rooms which are very clean and comfortable. All of the fixtures and flooring are new, so little of the building's historic character is visible from the inside, but the exterior boasts two old ruined towers which date from the last century. An effort has been made to preserve a historic feeling in the high-ceilinged dining room which is furnished with a large old oak armoire and table with rustic ladder-backed chairs. Breakfast is enjoyed either here, or, for a more leisurely morning, on the sunny back terrace overlooking a scenic view of the surrounding countryside. The five guest bedrooms are found upstairs and all have pretty arched windows and pleasant, if modest decor. *Directions:* Mancey is located approximately 6 kilometers west of Tournus. Leave Tournus on D14 in the direction of Charolles, continuing straight ahead on D215 towards Mancey. Just after the sign for the village of Mancey, but before actually entering the village centre, look for a gate on the left marked with a Chambres d'Hôtes sign. Go past the manor house on the hill, following an unpaved drive down the hill to the large stone farmhouse below.

CHEZ DEREPAS
Hostess: Madame Francoise Derepas
Dulphey, Mancey, 71240 Sennecey le Grand, France
tel: 85.51.10.22
5 Rooms, all with private shower, share 2 WC
Single: 115F, Double: 180F, Triple: 210F
No Table d'Hôte
Open all year
Good English spoken
Region: Burgundy

A real find, the Loisels' Georgian-style farmhouse is tastefully furnished with family antiques and pleasing colour combinations. The two high-ceilinged guest bedrooms have been recently redecorated in pretty flower print wallpapers, complemented by carpets and upholstery in soft colour tones. Bathrooms are scrupulously clean and well equipped. Downstairs in her dining room furnished in French country antiques, Madame Loisel serves delicious breakfasts and Table d'Hôte dinners featuring fresh farm produce. The imposing oak armoire and sideboard date from the time of her grandparents' marriage and add to the peaceful feeling of history and continuity that pervades Madame Loisel's lovely home. This pleasant B&B is enhanced by our energetic hostess who enjoys introducing her guests to regional dinner specialites and also teaches lacemaking and embroidery. *Directions:* Manneville la Goupil is located about 26 kilometers northeast of Le Havre via N15 to St Romain de Coulbosc, then D10 to Manneville la Goupil. Across from the church you will see a green and yellow Chambres d'Hôtes sign which directs you to turn left onto a small road leading out of town. About 1.5 kilometers later, turn right at the white fence which has a Gîtes de France sign posted on it.

CHEZ LOISEL
Hosts: Hubert and Nicole Loisel
Manneville la Goupil
76110 Goderville, France
tel: 35.27.77.21
3 Rooms, 2 with private bath/WC, others share bath/WC
Single: 130-180F, Double: 220F, Triple: 270F
Table d'Hôte: 90F
Open all year
No English spoken
Region: Normandy

Les Récollets is a stately manor home in the picturesque stone village of Marcigny. Originally a convent dating from 1724, this gracious country home has been in the Badin family for generations and is now a distinctive stopping place for travellers. The entire house is filled with lovely family antiques, rugs, paintings and objets d'art, creating a comfortably elegant ambiance. Bedrooms are all unique, each tastefully decorated in pretty colour schemes with complementing curtains and upholstery and furnished with beautiful family antiques and knicknacks. Many have pretty old fireplaces, high ceilings and tall windows which let in plenty of sunlight. Madame Badin is an attractive and vivacious hostess who takes great pleasure in pampering her guests and attending to thoughtful details such as bottled water and bouquets of fresh flowers in every room. *Directions:* Marcigny is located approximately 32 kilometers north of Roanne via D482. Once in the village, go to the Place du Champ de Foire (a square overlooking the countryside where the townsfolk gather to play boules) which is found at the edge of town on the road to Vichy. Iron gates marked by a Chambres d'Hôtes sign on the stone gatepost lead directly off the square into the Badins' front courtyard.

LES RÉCOLLETS
Hosts: Josette Badin
71110 Marcigny, France
tel: 85.25.05.16 fax: 85.25.06.91
9 Rooms, all with private bath/WC
Single: 300F, Double: 420F, Triple: 600F
Table d'Hôte: 200F per person
Open all year
Some English spoken
Region: South Burgundy

We received a warm welcome at Monsieur and Madame Bouteillers' charming half-timbered farmhouse where they have made their home for the last 40 years. Monsieur explained that he was originally a "city boy" from Rouen, but always wanted to be a farmer. He has achieved his dream in this pastoral setting where he and his wife have raised seven children   Madame's Table d'Hôte dinners always include regional specialties such as creamed chicken, duck with peach sauce and, of course, one of several varieties of homemade apple tarts.   These friendly meals are served in the light and cheerful entry salon with its long table   decorated with a wildflower bouquet in an earthenware jug. An antique sideboard and old stone mantel displaying pewter candlesticks add to the country ambiance. The Bouteillers' two guest rooms are clean and well equipped with simple decor and furnishings, including wooden beds and armoires. *Directions:* Martainville is located approximately 58 kilometers from Rouen via A13 to the Beuzeville exit. In Beuzeville, turn left at the traffic light at the church. Follow signs for the town of Épaignes via route D27. Approximately 3 kilometers later you will see a Chambres d'Hôtes sign directing you to turn right. A driveway on the left will then lead you to the Bouteillers' low, half-timbered farmhouse.

CHEZ BOUTEILLER
Hosts: Monsieur and Madame Jacques Bouteiller
Martainville, 27210 Beuzeville, France
tel: 32.57.82.23
2 Rooms, both with private bath/WC
Single: 150F, Double: 180F, Triple: 210F
Table d'Hôte: 70F per person
Open all year
Some English spoken by Monsieur
Region: Normandy

The small, out-of-the-way village of Maureilhan is a picturesque oasis of calm for travellers who like to get off the beaten track. A stay at the Fabre-Barthezes' comfortable home is a convivial, relaxing experience, a wonderful change from the commercial, impersonal atmosphere of many hotels. Monsieur and Madame are friendly winegrowers who produce rose and red wines in addition to welcoming bed and breakfast guests. They enjoy beginning an evening with a shared house aperitif, followed by a delicious four-course Table d'Hôte dinner and perhaps completed by a group sing-along. Meals are most often enjoyed in the small, tree-shaded garden where Madame grills savoury meats over grapevine branches. Peaceful bedrooms are located upstairs and are accessible through French doors from an outdoor balcony overlooking the courtyard and garden. Furnishings and decor are home-like and comfortable, with charming touches such as brass beds, crocheted coverlets and embroidered tablecloths. *Directions:* Maureilhan is located approximately 8 kilometers west of Béziers. Take N112 in the direction of St Pons until reaching the village of Maureilhan. Once in the village follow Chambres d'Hôtes signs to the second right turning, then right again under a stone archway to Fabre-Barthezes' courtyard.

CHEZ FABRE-BARTHEZ
Hosts: Monsieur and Madame Fabre-Barthez
7, rue Jean Jaures
Maureilhan, 34370 Cazouls les Béziers, France
tel: 67.90.52.49
6 Rooms, all w/pvt WC/shower or bath
Single: 145F, Double: 180F, Triple: 230F
Table d'Hôte: 70F per person
Open all year
No English spoken
Region: Languedoc-Roussillon

Le Moulin de Gennebrie is an old mill set in luxuriant countryside near Niort. The lush front garden of the ivy-covered building is filled with multicoloured flowers and banana palms. Breakfast is often enjoyed by the stream in the cool, grassy back grounds, shaded by tall poplars and weeping willow trees. Quiet and peaceful, Le Moulin de Gennebrie is truly an oasis in time and space. The guest entry is like a museum; through a cellar-like room and past the old mill wheel which still turns and produces electricity. Up two flights of rickety stairs, all the while observing the inner workings of the mill, guests finally arrive at the large unfinished attic area off which the three charming and tastefully decorated bedrooms are found. Pretty print fabrics and family antiques furnish the rooms, all of which share bath and WC. As parts of the mill are still in their unembellished original state, lodging here is recommended for travellers who seek character rather than up-to-date modern decor. *Directions:* Melle is located approximately 24 kilometers southeast of Niort. Take D948 to Melle, turning right onto D950 towards Brioux sur Boutonne. About 1 kilometer after passing the hamlet of Charzay, turn right and continue towards Perigne. After travelling a very short distance, about 1 kilometer, look for signs for Le Moulin de Gennebrie on the right.

* LE MOULIN DE GENNEBRIE
Hosts: Monsieur and Madame Merigeau
79500 Melle, France
tel: 49.07.11.96
3 Rooms, all share 1 separate WC and shower
Single: 120F, Double: 130F, Triple: 170F
No Table d'Hôte
Open May 1 to October 1
English spoken
n: Atlantic Coast

Bed & Breakfast Descriptions

Home-like Provencal charm abounds in the Derentys' contemporary villa located in an arid region of northern Provence. They built their house eight years ago in a typical regional style with a burnished tile roof and warm toned exterior walls, and an interior of cool tile floors and white plaster walls. Madame Derenty has decorated her guest bedrooms with curtains and bedspreads in the dainty and colourful prints typical of the Provence region and added pretty watercolours on the walls and some country antique furniture to create a fresh, feminine feeling throughout. A two-bedroom suite is offered in the main house, while an adjoining annex has two additional bedrooms, each with an independent entrance and private shower and WC. Breakfasts and Table d'Hôte dinners are usually enjoyed in the Derentys' quiet back garden and are friendly, family meals. A stay with the Derentys means modern comfort and fastidious attention to detail, as Madame Derenty is a solicitous hostess who makes sure her guests' every need is fulfilled. *Directions:* Mirabel aux Baronies is located approximately 4 kilometers south of Nyons via D538. Leave the village in the direction of Villedieu as directed by Chambres d'Hotes signs, and 1 kilometer later the Derentys' driveway will be on the left.

LA FOURNACHE
Hosts: Monsieur and Madame Derenty
Route de Villedieu
Mirabel aux Baronies, 26110 Nyons, France
tel: 75.27.14.83
3 Rooms, 2 with private WC, bath or shower
Single: 195F, Double: 320F, Triple: 435F
Rates include breakfast & dinner
Open all year
Some English spoken by husband
Region: Provence

An unprepossessing entrance through a small arched gateway leads to the modest Ferme Auberge des Noyers. The cosy restaurant has exposed stone walls, a large fireplace and intimate seating at six tables dressed with rose-coloured tablecloths and napkins topped by white lace. Madame Galy serves old-fashioned cuisine utilizing fresh farm meats and vegetables while Monsieur attends mainly to his primary occupation as a wine-grower. Their regional red wine can be purchased or enjoyed with dinner specialties such as rabbit cooked over a wood fire and savory bean and meat stews. The bedrooms are all very basic and plain in their furnishings, with small, but adequate, bathroom facilities. Most rooms have their own French door providing access from an outdoor terrace. In order to keep the summer heat under control, the rooms are windowless with thick stucco walls, cool tile floors and heavy shutters over the French doors. A refreshing blue swimming pool offers a pleasant escape on hot days. *Directions:* Montbrun des Corbières is located about 35 kilometers east of Carcassonne. Take N113 towards Narbonne, turning left after about 20 kilometers towards Montbrun des Corbières. In the village, follow signs for Ferme Auberge.

AUBERGE DES NOYERS
Hosts: Monsieur and Madame Galy
Montbrun des Corbières, 11700 Capendu, France
tel: 68.43.94.01
5 Rooms all with private shower/WC
Single: 160F, Double: 180F, Triple: 260F
Table d'Hôte: 85-145F per person
Open Easter to October 15,
  And weekends all year
Some English spoken
Region: Languedoc-Roussillon

Montchavin is a picturesque mountain town of Alpine chalets and narrow, winding streets. In winter, skiers flock here for intimate lodging and dining near the major ski area of La Plagne. Monsieur and Madame Favre are a friendly, attractive young couple who run the convivial La Bovate restaurant and also offer guest accommodation. Guests enjoy regional dishes such as beef and cheese fondues in the rustic dining room built with dark wood panelling, beamed ceilings and a large stone fireplace. A pretty annex houses guest rooms which are clean and fresh, featuring natural wood walls and furniture. There is also an apartment and even a separate chalet with its own garden and terrace, fireplace and well-equipped kitchen. *Directions:* Montchavin is located about 100 kilometers east of Chambéry. From Chambéry follow directions for Albertville on N90. At Albertville, continue towards Moutiers, Bourg St Maurice, then 1 kilometer after the village of Bellentre, look for a turnoff for Landry, Montchavin les Cloches. Follow a winding road up a hillside, following signs for Montchavin. Enter the village of Montchavin le Plan through an archway and continue straight up the main street, veering to the right once the streets become twisty. The road will narrow and basically come to an end in a little square: look for La Bovate on the right.

LA BOVATE
Hosts: Michèle and Fortuné Favre
Montchavin, 73210 Bellentre, France
tel: 79.07.83.25
1 Room, 5 Apartments, 1 Chalet, all w/private bath
Single: 200F, Double: 240F, Triple: 290F
Table d'Hôte: moderately priced restaurant
Open Summer and Winter
Some English spoken
Region: French Alps

The Chateau de Montmaur is a designated historic monument dating from the 14th century.   Found in a small village surrounded by tree-covered hills and mountains, the castle is built on a grand scale, with thick stone walls and two great halls. Authentic wood floors, fresco paintings and huge fireplaces all testify to the castle's colourful past as a fortress, a royal castle and even a headquarters for resistance fighters during World War II.   The Laurens family are dedicated to breathing life into their historic home and have opened the large halls to public tours, weddings, classical music concerts, receptions and parties.   Parts of the castle are still being restored and five intimate suites have recently been completed for bed and breakfast guests.   The rooms are prettily decorated with elegant fabrics and wallpapers and each has private shower and WC as well as an independent entrance.   Breakfast is served in the Laurens' charming salon/dining room which has a beamed ceiling and a lovely stone fireplace and is decorated with country antiques and fresh flower bouquets. *Directions:* Montmaur is located approximately 17 kilometers west of Gap.   Take D994 towards Veynes, then about 4 kilometers after the town of Roche des Arnauds, turn to the right following signs for Montmaur.   The castle gate is clearly marked at the entry to the village.

CHATEAU DE MONTMAUR
Hosts: Monsieur and Madame Laurens
Montmaur, 05400 Veynes, France
tel: 92.58.11.42
5 Suites, with private shower/WC
Single: 300F, Double: 400F, Triple: 480F
Table d'Hôte: 100F
Open all year
No English spoken
Region: French Alps

With so many of the places in the Loire Valley extremely expensive, it is a pleasure to recommend the well-priced Manoir de la Salle, an attractive bed & breakfast tucked into the hillside above the river Cher. Terraced gardens buffer it from any street noise below and enhance the views from the patio. The grounds boast a tennis court, a rose garden, ponds and shaded lawns that tempt one to sit and relax after a day of sightseeing. The manor house was recently purchased by the Boussard family who are continuing with the same gracious welcome as the previous owners who also opened their home as a bed and breakfast. Guest rooms are found both in the tower and in the main building. They vary in size, but all have a private bathroom and are decorated with family furnishings and are thoughtfully appointed. Guests are made to feel as if the manor is their home for the duration of their stay. Breakfast is served in the dining room where guests have the chance to meet and talk to fellow travellers. The Manoir de la Salle is located just to the south of Chaumont and east of Chenonceaux, an ideal base for touring the chateaux of the Loire Valley. *Directions:* From Montrichard travel D176 east for approximately three kilometers to the village of Bourre. The Manoir de la Salle is signposted just beyond the village of Bourre, above the road.

MANOIR DE LA SALLE
Hosts: Monsieur and Madame Boussard
69, route de Vierzon
Bourre, 41400 Montrichard
tel: 54.32.73.54
4 rooms, all with private bath
Double: 450F to 650F
Table d'Hôte: check with owner
Open Easter to November
Some English spoken by M. Boussard
Region: Loire Valley

Chateau le Goupillon is an imposing chateau found in a tranquil setting in the open countryside. Madame Calot is the independent, energetic hostess who has used her artistic talents to renovate her grand home, creating a home-like rather than elegant feeling in her guest rooms and public areas. Orange walls, a parquet floor and country antique furniture lend a warm, comfortable feeling to the dining room where breakfast is enjoyed. Bedrooms are large and airy, with high ceilings and bright, earth-toned colour schemes. Handcrafted macrame and weaving warm the walls. Furniture is a mix of antique and modern, but all is comfortable and spacious. Two adjoining bedrooms, one with double bed and one with two twins, form a suite that is perfect for families. Madame has even supplied toys in the children's room. Guests are welcome to relax in the downstairs salon, casually furnished with family antiques and inviting couches and chairs, or on the front terrace which looks out over a long expanse of green lawn bordered by tall trees. *Directions:* Neuille is located 8 kilometers north of Saumur. Take N147 from Saumur to D767 in the direction of Vernantes le Lude. After passing a miniature golf course, turn left onto D129 towards Neuille. Look for Chambres d'Hôtes signs which will lead directly to Madame Calot's driveway.

CHATEAU LE GOUPILLON
Hostess: Madame Calot
Neuille, 49680 Vivy, France
tel: 41.52.51.89
2 Rooms, 1 Suite,
All with private bath or shower & WC
Single: 230-380F, Double: 290-440F
No Table d'Hôte
Open April 1 to November 1
No English spoken
Region: Loire Valley

Madame Gourlaouen enjoys a tranquil location near the spectacular coastline and beaches of southern Brittany and the artist community of Pont Aven. This picturesque port town is the former home of many French impressionist painters, as well as Paul Gauguin. Madame Gourlaouen is a young, capable hostess who offers bed and breakfast as well as apartment accommodation in her pretty stone farmhouse. Dating from 1730, the long, low house is built from the golden-hued stones which are typical of the Concarneau, Pont Aven region. An independent entrance leads to the guest bedrooms which are furnished with antique reproductions. Rooms are small but charming and all have private WC and shower. The intimate breakfast room is full of charm with a low, beamed ceiling, old stone hearth, country antiques and fresh garden flowers. *Directions:* Nevez is located approximately 30 kilometers southeast of Quimper. Leave the town of Pont Aven on D70 towards Concarneau, turning left just outside town following signs to Nevez. In the village of Nevez, continue past the church, then take the left fork in the road onto D77 towards Port Manech. After about 4 kilometers, just before entering Port Manech, look for a Chambres d'Hôtes sign directing you to turn right. Continue following signs, turning at the first left, and you will arrive at this sunny farmhouse 300 metres from the sea.

CHEZ GOURLAOUEN
Hostess: Madame Yveline Gourlaouen
Port Manech, Kerambris, 29920 Nevez, France
tel: 98.06.83.82
6 Rooms, all with private shower/WC
Single: 170F, Double: 200F
No Table d'Hôte
Open all year
Some English spoken
Region: Brittany

A modest, contemporary home in a quiet, pastoral suburb of Niort is the setting for bed and breakfast accommodation Chez Boudreault. A spacious, well-landscaped garden and lawn surround the home, with a refreshing swimming pool adding a touch of luxury. The guest bedroom is adequately furnished with somewhat basic, old-fashioned decor, but is highly comfortable and adjacent to a modern, private bathroom. Welcome details such as a large bath, double basins and good lighting are supplemented by thoughtfully supplied soap and fluffy towels. Breakfast is served in the family kitchen and is basic Continental fare. The Boudreaults are friendly hosts and have two teenage children who speak a very small amount of English. Chez Boudreault is recommended primarily as a convenient stopover as it is close to the main road, reasonably priced and provides a warm and personal family welcome. *Directions:* Chez Boudreault is in the village of Surimeau which is located approximately 3 kilometers north of Niort. Leave Niort on D743 in the direction of Parthenay. After travelling about 1 kilometer, look for a used car lot on the right and take the road opposite, on the left, which leads to Surimeau. The Bourdreaults' house is the first on the right: 27, rue de Mineraie.

CHEZ BOUDREAULT
Hosts: Monsieur and Madame Boudreault
27, rue de Mineraie
Surimeau, 79000 Niort, France
tel: 49.24.51.93
1 Room with private bath
Single: 120F, Double: 150F
Table d'Hôte: 50F per person
  (by reservation only)
Open all year
Very little English spoken
Region: Atlantic Coast

The magical forested hills surrounding the village of Obersteinbach are dotted with ruins of ancient medieval fortresses: mystical remnants of the region's feudal past. Carved from the red sandstone rock formations and overgrown with vines and wildflowers, with ancient doors, walls and windows still easily visible, they offer a fascinating glimpse back to the 13th century. Maison Ullmann is a truly special place to stay and an ideal base for hikers; near many mountain paths leading through enchanted pine and deciduous forests. Local historian and nature lover Cristelle and her husband Jean are warm, relaxed hosts who enjoy introducing their guests to the wonders of the surrounding countryside and the region's rich past. Their garden is a medieval delight featuring herbs and roses. Bedrooms are furnished with charming simplicity and artistic flair, providing comfortable, home-like accommodation with a kitchenette in every room. *Directions:* Obersteinbach is located about 60 km north of Strasbourg, very near the German border. Travel north on N83 to Hagenau, continuing in the direction of Wissembourg until just outside of town where you will pick up D27 past Woerth to Lembach. Veer left onto D3 and continue to Niedersteinbach and Obersteinbach. Traverse the village on the main street (rue Principale) and look for Maison Ullmann on the left.

MAISON ULLMANN
Hosts: Jean and Cristelle Zerafa
62, rue Principale
67510 Obersteinbach, France
tel: 88.09.50.47 fax: 88.09.53.56
5 Rooms, all w/pvt WC/bath or shower
Single: 245F, Double: 280F, Triple: 340F
Table d'Hôte: 65F
Open all year except January
Good English spoken, also fluent German
Region: Alsace

Madame Benech is a widow who lives on a peaceful farm in the hills of Auvergne where she offers camping in her front garden and bed and breakfast accommodation in her pretty stone farmhouse. Guest bedrooms are simply and comfortably equipped with old-fashioned furniture and neutral colour schemes. Bathroom facilities are shared, but each room has its own basin. Breakfast is served downstairs in the inviting dining room at a long wooden table in front of a large open-hearthed fireplace. Charming touches are added by hanging copper pots, red geraniums at the windows and country antiques. Chez Benech is recommended for travellers who do not mind shared bath facilities and are seeking practical, very clean accommodation at reasonable prices. The Auvergne region is lovely and unspoilt, offering endless opportunities for hiking and exploring medieval castles and villages. *Directions:* Olmet is located approximately 14 kilometers east of Aurillac. Take N122 towards Vic sur Cere and Murat. At the small settlement of Comblat, turn right onto D57 to Olmet and Aris. Once in the hamlet of Olmet, look for a Chambres d'Hôtes sign directing you to turn right up a country lane. Madame Benech's two-storey white house is on the right, set back from the road behind a green field usually occupied by some campers and tents.

* CHEZ BENECH
Hostess: Madame Benech
Olmet, 15800 Vic sur Cère, France
tel: 71.47.50.54
4 Rooms, none with private bath
Single: 90F, Double: 145F
No Table d'Hôte
Open February 1 to September 15
Very little English spoken
Region: Auvergne

The small village of Ordonnaz, tucked away in the hilly, forested countryside, is the peaceful setting for La Ferme Auberge Le Charveyron where the Laracine family offers home-like guest accommodation and delicious, farm-fresh meals. They make all their own pastries and breads and serve savoury local specialties in their rustically cosy dining rooms or on a pretty outdoor terrace overlooking the surrounding hills. One guest bedroom in the Laracines' home offers basic accommodation with bath facilities common to the family, and for travellers seeking a higher level of privacy and comfort, a newly built annex offers three bedrooms, each with private shower and WC. *Directions:* Ordonnaz is located approximately 50 kilometers west of Aix les Bains. From Aix, loop around the southern end of the lake on N201 and N211 and pick up N504 following signs for Belley, Amberieu en Bugey and Bourg en Bresse. Continue about 9 kilometers past Belley to the small village of Pugieu. On the main street, look carefully for a turnoff to the left for Contrevoz. Follow this lovely country lane which winds up through trees and green pastures through Contrevoz and on to Ordonnaz. Once in the village, go to the central fountain and veer left. The Laracines' home is on the right and easily recognizable by the table umbrellas on the front terrace.

LA FERME AUBERGE
Hosts: Monsieur and Madame Rene Laracine
01510 Ordonnaz, France
tel: 74.36.42.38
3 Rooms, All with private shower/WC
Single: 180F, Double: 200F
Ferme Auberge: 60-80F
Open all year
Very little English spoken
Region: French Alps

The lovely Chauveau home enjoys an idyllic setting on a hillside overlooking the family vineyards and the distant River Vienne. The fine art of relaxing is easy to master in these luxurious and scenic surroundings where each day begins with fresh croissants and coffee or tea on the terrace overlooking the lush valley. Impeccable taste prevails in the furnishings and decor, creating an elegant country home ambiance. Madame Chauveau offers two bedrooms in her home as well as a two-bedroom poolside suite. The suite is very handsome with stone walls, slate tile floors and pretty country antique furniture. Sunny yellow print curtains and matching upholstery complete the pleasing ensemble. The Chauveaus' pool and sunbathing terrace is only steps away; perfect for an early morning dip. Guest bedrooms in the main house are furnished in highly tasteful combinations of designer fabrics in floral motifs complemented by charming old paintings, antique chests and beds. A stay at Domaine de Beauséjour is truly an experience to be savoured. *Directions:* Panzoult is located approximately 12 kilometers east of Chinon. Take D21 in the direction of L'Île Bouchard through the village of Panzoult. Two kilometers out of town there is a sign marking the driveway of Domaine de Beauséjour to the right - the pretty, light stone house on the edge of the woods.

DOMAINE DE BEAUSÉJOUR
Hosts: Marie-Claude and Gérard Chauveau
Panzoult, 37220 L'Ile Bouchard, France
tel: 47.58.64.64
4 Rooms, 2 with private bath/WC
Single: 250F, Double: 400F, Triple: 500F
No Table d'Hôte
Open all year
Good English spoken
Region: Loire Valley

Life in the French countryside is at its casual, relaxed best at Les Granges. Hostess Madame Kling-Bienvenu is American born, although her father was French, so she speaks fluent English. A former fashion model, Madame Kling-Bienvenu welcomes photography crews and models on fashions shoots as well as bed and breakfast guests to her country manor home. The interior is decorated in an attractive, uncluttered, less-is-more style, creating a simple, yet elegant ambiance. Guest bedrooms and public areas are entirely furnished in lovely antiques, complemented by well-chosen artwork, Oriental rugs and fabrics. Many of the bedrooms contain rich details such as original tile floors and working fireplaces. Outdoors, a sunny back terrace looks out over an expanse of green lawn bordered by a tall hedge which screens a swimming pool. *Directions:* Parçay is located about 40 kilometers south of Tours. Take autoroute A10 exiting at St Maure and turn onto D760 travelling in the direction of L'Îsle Bouchard and Richlieu. After 3 kilometers, turn left onto D58 to Pouzay. Go through town and just after crossing the bridge over the Vienne River, turn right onto D18 to Parçay sur Vienne. Before reaching the village, follow signs which direct to Les Granges. Continue down the driveway past the old farm to Madame Kling-Bienvenu's large, blue-shuttered house.

* LES GRANGES
Hostess: Madame Kling-Bienvenu
Parçay sur Vienne
37220 L'Isle Bouchard, France
tel: 47.58.54.62 (winter months: 1.47.20.54.50)
5 Rooms, all with private WC, 2 share bath
Single: 250F, Double: 450F
Table d'Hôte: 120F per person
Open June 1 to November 1
Fluent English spoken
Region: Loire Valley

The romantic L'Ormeraie, secreted on a tiny lane in a splendid untouristy area of southwest France, is owned by the charming Michel de l'Ormeraie. It took him over 20 years to transform the neglected 17th-century farmhouse into the dream it is today - a picture perfect, mellow stone farmhouse accented with white shutters and climbing roses. There are five guest rooms: my choice is the "Chambre du Parc", a spacious room, nicely decorated with antiques and with French doors opening onto the garden. But, the favorite place of all is the terrace where guests can relax and enjoy a scene of utter tranquility looking out over the sloping pastures to forested hills. A path leads down from the terrace to a small circular swimming pool nestled on the lawn. Whereas many of the places we saw in France has a bit of a ramshackle look about them, Michel has managed to achieve an informality about his little farm yet maintain a beautifully groomed, carefully tended look both to his house and his lovely rose and flower gardens. *Directions:* Agen is located 140 km southeast of Bordeaux via the A62 / E72. From Agen go north on N21 to Villeneuve and take D676 northeast to Monflanquin. Then take D272 northeast 7 km to Laussou and turn right on the narrow road 161 toward Bonnenouvelle. L'Ormeraie is about 1.5 km down 161 on your right.

L'ORMERAIE
Host: Michel de l'Ormeraie
Laussou, 47150 Paulhiac, France
tel: 53.36.45.96
5 Rooms, all with private bath/WC
Single: 255-305F, Double: 260-480F, Triple: 480-555F
Table d'Hôte: 130F per person
Credit cards: None
Open Easter to November 15
Very little English spoken
Region: Lot and Garonne

Veal farmers Janine and Charles Lacaze have recently converted their historic barn into comfortable guest accommodation. A large arched doorway leads into a spacious guest kitchen and dining area with exposed stone walls and a stone fireplace. Upstairs, the five recently remodelled guest bedrooms are fresh and inviting with reproduction antique furniture and dainty floral print wallpapers. Janine is a scrupulous housekeeper who makes sure linens are fresh and rooms spotless. Skylight windows look out over the wooded hills and let in the pure country air. Breakfast is served in the Lacazes' farmhouse, a pretty stone structure dating from the early 1800s which has been in Charles's family for three generations. Fresh coffee and croissants are enjoyed at a long table in the low-ceilinged dining room before an arched stone fireplace. The charming scene is completed by hanging copper pots, exposed stone walls and a friendly collie dog asleep by the hearth. *Directions:* Pers is a very small village located about 25 kilometers west of Aurillac. Take N122 south towards Toulouse. After about 18 kilometers, turn right towards Pers. The road forks several times; keep following signs pointing to Pers. Go through the village and look for a Chambres d'Hôtes sign at the far edge, indicating a driveway on the left.

FERME DE VIESCAMP
Hosts: Janine and Charles Lacaze
15290 Pers, France
tel: 71.62.25.14
5 Rooms, all with private shower or bath/WC
Single: 148F, Double: 171F, Triple: 234F
No Table d'Hôte
Open April 15 to November 15
No English spoken, fluent Spanish spoken
Region: Auvergne

Monsieur and Madame Colin are renovating a home in the village of Plaissan which they have opened as a bed and breakfast.　When we visited all of the work had not been completed, but two of the guest rooms were ready and the third one was almost completed.　The house had obviously been at one time the home of a wealthy family - the Colins are restoring many of the special features such as fancy tiled floors, marble walls, hand-painting on the walls and fancy chandeliers.　On the first floor is the dining room with a handsome oak dining table.　Upstairs are the bedrooms.　The most expensive one is a suite with the bathroom dividing the room into two sleeping areas, however, I preferred the less expensive rooms: my favorite one faces the park and has a handsome antique bed.　Although this home offers simple accommodation, it is inviting, pleasantly furnished and efficiently managed.　*Directions:* Plaissan is located 42 km west of Montpellier.　Drive southwest from Montpellier on the A9 for 21 km.　Then take the Sete exit and go north on D2 via Poussan.　As you drive into town, turn right at the Gîte sign (rue des Prunus) and go 3 blocks.　The house is located on the left side of the street, on the corner of des Prunus and rue de L'Aire, across the street from the park.

CHEZ COLIN
Hosts: Monsieur and Madame Colin
Rue des Prunus (1, rue de L'Aire)
34230 Plaissan, France
tel: 67.96.81.16
3 Rooms, all with private bath/WC
Single: 175F, Double: 180-195F, Triple: 230F
No Table d'Hôte, restaurant nearby
Credit cards: None
Open all year
No English spoken
Region: Languedoc-Rousillon

Bed & Breakfast Descriptions

Two years ago Even O'Neill gave up a high-powered role in the business world in order to take on that of host in his family's 15th century manor house hotel. His deep love for his heritage shows in every aspect of his solicitous management of the Manoir de Vaumadeuc. All the rooms have been renovated and redecorated under Even's direction, ushering in a new era of freshness and elegant style to the ancient medieval surroundings. In spite of the thick stone walls and huge walk-in fireplaces, the feeling throughout is light, airy and very comfortable. The guestrooms in the main house are very large with high ceilings and fireplaces. Lovely floral fabrics, paintings and antiques lend a luxurious, yet personalized atmosphere. There are also two cottage style bedrooms located in the carriage house which are smaller and thus cosier than those in the manoir. Delicious dinners are graciously served in the intimate restaurant by personable Even and his wife Carol. Located twelve miles from Brittany's coast in the Hunaudaye Forest, the manoir reflects an ambiance of beauty, gentility and peace. *Directions:* From Plancoët, take D768 towards Lamballe. 1 km later, go left on D28 for about 7 km to the village of Pléven. Go through the village and you will see the Manoir de Vaumadeuc on the right.

MANOIR DE VAUMADEUC
Hosts: Even and Carol O'Neill
Pleven 22130 Plancoët
tel: 96.84.46.17 fax: 96.84.40.16
10 rooms/suites, all with pvt bath
Single: 490F Double: 490-850F Triple: 700-950F
Dinner: price varies
Open March 15-January 5
Good English spoken
Region: Brittany

L'Estel, located in the heart of Provence, is a small B&B that might well appeal to you, especially if your are travelling with small children and would like to practice your high school French.   The handsome, most gracious young owner, Pierre-Jean Turion, showed us around the inn while his pretty wife was in the kitchen caring for the children who will be the 5th generation to live in this 200-year old farm house. The farmhouse is located right on the main road, but a high stone fence creates a nucleus of privacy for the pretty walled garden where breakfast is served each morning.   Pierre-Jean said that the wall is going to be extended and a swimming pool tucked onto the property.   A central room, bright and cheerful with lots of sunlight streaming through large windows, is attractively decorated by antique groupings of tables and chairs.   Upstairs are 5 absolutely immaculate bedrooms. Several of them have small lofts where, if you are travelling with children, they would love to sleep.   Jacqueline, upon prior notice, cooks dinner for her guests. *Directions:* Pont du Gard is located 25 km west of Avignon.   From Remoulins take D 981 following signs to Uzes.   After about 3km you will see the Gite sign on your right, drive in and park.   L'Estel is located on the main road D981.

L'ESTEL
Hosts: Jacqueline & Pierre-Jean Turion
La Begude de Vers
30210 Pont due Gard, France
tel: 66.37.18.11
5 Rooms, 5 with private bath/WC
Single: 180F, Double: 280F, Triple: 330F
Table d'Hôte: 70F per person
Credit cards: None accepted
Open all year
No English spoken
Region: Provence

Conveniently located for sightseeing in the interior of Brittany, the Chateau de Pontgamp offers guests luxurious accommodation in an old Breton manor home. Monsieur Pourdieu is your gracious host who happily shares his extensive knowledge of the region, helps plan walking tours and even offers lessons in the traditional Breton method of cooking crepes.   Perched on a hillside above the town of Pontgamp, the Pourdieu home is furnished with many elegant antiques, and offers almost every comfort imaginable for guests including televisions, private baths and writing desks.   Decor is very attractive; soft toned wallpapers and carpets in harmonious colours.   *Directions:* The village of Pontgamp adjoins the village of Plouguenast and is located approximately 38 kilometers south of St Brieuc.   If approaching from the north, drive through Plouguenast and turn left at the first street after the bridge over the river.   At this point you can see the Chateau de Pontgamp on the hill above.   The driveway is on the left.

CHATEAU DE PONTGAMP
Host: Monsieur Pourdieu
Pontgamp
22150 Plouguenast, France
tel: 96.28.71.99
2 Suites, both with private bath
Double: 250-300F, Triple: 380F
No Table d'Hôte
Open all year
Very little English spoken
Region: Brittany

Drive down a country lane past a field of sunflowers to arrive in the tiny hamlet of La Galeze, where friendly hosts Denise and Pierre Billat extend a warm welcome to their peaceful country home.   The front garden is a glorious profusion of colourful flowers, blackberry brambles and sweet-smelling herbs; bordered by a hedge which conceals a large garden full of healthy vegetables.   Nearby woods and countryside offer many footpaths for long walks or bike rides.   Adjoining the main house is an inviting stone room once used for distilling cognac, now renovated into a cosy guest salon.   Ther is also a dining room where Denise and Pierre share delicious and convivial home-cooked meals with their guests.   Guest rooms vary in size; the ground-floor bedrooms are spacious and have private baths, while the attic rooms are smaller, with shared bath facilities.   All the rooms are tastefully decorated in a simple country style with details such as lace curtains and flowering plants adding Denise's personal, feminine touch.   *Directions:* Pouillac is located approximately 50 kilometers northeast of Bordeaux.   Take N10 north in the direction of Angoulême just past the town of Montlieu la Garde to Pouillac.   Go through the village and turn left, following directions for the hamlet of La Galèze.   One kilometer later look for a Chambres d'Hôtes sign on the right indicating a short driveway to the Billats' picturesque home.

LA THÉBAÏDE
Hosts: Denise and Pierre Billat
La Galèze - Pouillac, 17210 Montlieu la Garde,France
tel: 46.04.65.17
4 Rooms, 3 w/private bath, 1 w/private shower
Single: 135-160F, Double: 180-210F, Triple: 245F
Table d'Hôte: 65-70F per person
Open all year
No English spoken
Region: Atlantic Coast

Monsieur and Madame Line are an attractive, hospitable couple who take great pleasure in welcoming guests to their charming home in the countryside. The Lines enjoy inviting their guests to share an aperitif in their airy glassed-in veranda looking out over their peaceful back garden and tennis court. An independent entrance leads upstairs to the three pretty bedrooms which are furnished with highly polished antique beds, chests and armoires and complementing designer wallpapers, upholstery and curtains. Breakfast is a special treat at the Lines', as they serve a copious meal complete with a special goat cheese from their nearby farm. The country breakfast room is indeed a pleasant place to linger, with its old tiled floor and stone fireplace, country antiques and pewter collection. This is a bed and breakfast that tops our list; including all the elements of comfort, reasonable price, charming decor, atmosphere and an open-hearted welcome. *Directions:* Pussigny is located about 22 kilometers north of Chatellerault. Take N10 north in the direction of Tours, turn left at the village of Port de Piles in the direction of Marigny, then, just after crossing the River Vienne, turn left again in the direction of Pussigny. Just after entering the village limits, look for a Chambres d'Hôtes sign and the Lines' warm stone house on the left.

LE CLOS SAINT-CLAIR
Hosts: Monsieur and Madame Line
Pussigny, 37800 Ste Maure de Touraine, France
tel: 47.65.01.27
3 Rooms, all with private shower/WC
Single: 145F, Double: 200-230F, Triple: 260-290F
No Table d'Hôte
Open all year
Very little English spoken
Region: Loire Valley

A circular drive, soft green lawn and brightly painted blue door welcome guests into the imposing home of Monsieur and Madame Rogoff. The Rogoffs are a farming family who have raised three children here in this pleasant manor house. Decor is home-like rather than elegant, with bright touches such as colorful lamps and fresh flower bouquets. Madame enjoys crafts and her handiwork is evident in the crocheted bedspreads and dried flower wreaths which add personality to the bedrooms. The downstairs bedroom is very spacious with a private bath/WC located across the hall. Upstairs, a very pretty room with country antique furniture shares a WC in the hall but has a private adjoining bath. Breakfast is served at a long table in Madame's sunny country kitchen where a fire warms the hearth on cool mornings. The front garden offers a peaceful retreat after a day of sightseeing in nearby Bayeux, well known for its collection of beautiful tapestries - the most famous of which depicts the Battle of Hastings. *Directions:* Ranchy is located 2 kilometers southwest of Bayeux via D5 towards le Molay Littry, turning left after 1 kilometer onto D169 to Ranchy. There is a sign for another Chambres d'Hôtes just before entering the village of Ranchy, so be sure to continue into town where you will see a second Chambres d'Hôtes sign directing you to the Rogoffs' gate.

CHEZ ROGOFF
Hosts: Monsieur and Madame Rogoff
Ranchy 14400 Bayeux, France
tel: 31.92.36.42
2 Rooms, both w/private bath, one shares WC
Single: 110F, Double: 160F
No Table d'Hôte
Open all year
No English spoken
Region: Normandy

If you are looking for a wonderful castle, absolutely brimming with character, tucked far from the maddening crowds, the Chateau de Regagnac is your dream come true. The road to the castle winds through a forest and finally deadends at the Chateau de Regagnac. Go through the gates and into the courtyard which extends to a bluff and offers a sensational view out to forrested hills. Chateau de Regagnac is totally furnished in family antiques - although the decor is stunning, there is a homey ambiance - nothing seems stiff or formal. Some of the bedrooms are in the main part of the castle and others in across the courtyard, but it does not matter which you reserve, they are all beautiful. Serge Pardoux is a great collector: don't miss seeing his stunning collection of lead soldiers. Mme Pardoux is a superb cook, and with advance reservation, will prepare a gourmet meal for you - the price is not inexpensive, but the meal will be memorable. Serge Pardoux is the epitome of graciousness who says that "once a person walks through the gates, he is becomes a friend, a guest in my home." *Directions:* Bergerac is located about 87 km east of Bordeaux via the D936. Head east from Bergerac on D660 for 27 km to Beaumont. Then take D25 east to Cadouin and turn right on D2 toward Monpazier; then take the 3rd small road on the left and follow signs to Regagnac.

CHATEAU DE REGAGNAC
Hosts: M & Mme Serge Pardoux
Regagnac, 24440 Beaumont, France
tel: 53.53.27.02
5 Rooms, all with private bath/WC
Double: 500F
Table d'Hôte: 400F per person, prior notice
Credit cards: None accepted
Open all year
Fluent English spoken
Region: Périgord

Monsieur and Madame Vandel recently purchased the magnificent Chateau de Reignac, once a residence of famous French general La Fayette, and have lovingly refurbished and redecorated it in highly authentic 17th-century style.   The Vandels are antique dealers and part of the castle houses their well-stocked showroom where guests are welcome to browse among their many treasures.   Perfection is a key word at Chateau de Reignac and Madame and Monsieur, along with their daughter and two sons, are friendly hosts who attend to the smallest details with indefatigable energy.   All of the beautifully preserved and furnished public rooms are open to guests and contain museum-quality decor including crystal chandeliers and original carved wood ceilings.   Guest breakfasts are served in the oldest part of the castle; the former soldiers' quarters, dating from the 11th century. Bedrooms are all elegant works of art, displaying period furniture and artifacts and wallpapers which are copies of old designs.   Even the bathrooms provide a taste of the past, as each contains an old-fashioned clawfoot bathtub. *Directions:* Reignac sur Indre is located approximately 22 kilometers southeast of Tours. Take N143 towards Loches, turning left after about 20 kilometers onto D58 to Reignac.   Once in the village, look for the castle gate across from the church.

CHATEAU DE REIGNAC
Hosts: Monsieur and Madame Vandel
37310 Reignac sur Indre, France
tel: 47.94.14.10
7 Rooms, all w/pvt WC/bath or shower
Single: 300F, Double: 600F, Triple: 900F
No Table d'Hôte
Open all year
Some English spoken
Region: Loire Valley

Madame Le Platre's elegant town home enjoys a central, picturesque location on La Place des Religieuses in the small town of Richelieu. This entire town is classified as an historical monument and is the former site of Cardinal Richelieu's magnificent castle and estate. Madame Le Platre is a local history buff who is happy to share her extensive knowledge with her guests and help them plan sightseeing excursions. Her own home dates from 1638 and is like a modest museum with its antique furnishings, decor and collections. All of her inviting bedrooms are decorated in a refined, old-fashioned style. Madame also offers an adorable little apartment across the rear courtyard where guests have a small downstairs sitting area and two bedrooms. The larger bedroom has a beautiful dark red tile floor and is furnished with impressive old paintings and antique furniture, while the smaller bedroom is furnished in a very cute manner with a blue checked cloth forming a canopy over the bed. On warm mornings breakfast can be enjoyed in the tranquil courtyard at an outdoor table. *Directions:* Richelieu is located approximately 55 kilometers northwest of Chatellerault. Take A10 to the St Maure de la Touraine exit, then follow signs for Richelieu. You will enter the town via La Place des Réligieuses and Madame Le Platre's house is number 24.

CHEZ LE PLATRE
Hostess: Madame Marie Josèphe Le Platre
1, rue Jarry, 37120 Richelieu, France
tel: 47.58.10.42
4 Rooms, all with private shower/WC
Single: 200F, Double: 220F, Triple: 320F
No Table d'Hôte
Open all year
No English spoken
Region: Loire Valley

Le Moulin des Chézeaux is a picture-perfect 14th-century flour mill, painted white with delft-blue shutters, and red geraniums spilling from boxes at every window. Adding to the story-book ambiance is a small lake (with ducks, of course) and a stream. Inside, the enchantment continues. In any one of the three guest rooms you will feel a bit like you are "living" in a stage setting - superb fabrics, antique furniture, fresh flowers everywhere and the finest of linens. The creation of this elegant little B&B was the handiwork of Ren Rijpstra (a talented interior designer) and Willem Prinsloo (a successful business consultant). Their genuine warmth of welcome combined with a boundless desire to pamper their guests makes one feel like royalty. Ren, is not only a clever decorator, but a fabulous chef - be sure to reserve for dinner. A few steps away, Ren and Willem have beautifully restored and decorated a 3 bedroom, 2 bath, 300-year-old stone cottage (for weekly rentals). Note: no smoking, no children under 10. *Directions:* Rivarennes is located 76 km east of Poitiers. From Poitiers take N151 east. Just west of St. Gaultier, exit north on D46 toward Migne. Turn right at the first road, then left at the second road which immediately splits. Follow the right hand lane down to the mill.

LE MOULIN DES CHÉZEAUX
Hosts: Ren Rijpstra & Willem Prinsloo
Rivarennes
36800 St Gaultier, France
tel: 54.47.01.84 fax: 54.01.15.88
3 Rooms, all with private bath/WC
Double: 300-400F, House: 3,000F-4,000F/week
Table d'Hôte: from 110F per person, prior notice
Credit cards: None
Open January to December
Fluent English spoken
Region: Limousin

Les Salles is recommended for travellers seeking basic, modern comfort and a high degree of cleanliness rather than historic ambiance. Conveniently located near the scenic river canyons Gorges du Tarn, the Meljacs' newly built house of light-toned regional stone is surrounded by Monsieur's family vineyards. They produce a red table wine which accompanies their Table d'Hôte dinners featuring fresh garden vegetables. The home-like guest dining room is furnished in rustic reproduction furniture accented by bright red tablecloths and has French doors which lead out to a peaceful front terrace. Simple, family-style meals and hospitality are offered at Les Salles. The bedrooms are furnished mainly in rattan furniture and are somewhat stark in their decor, with cool white walls and tile floors. A refreshing swimming pool is a welcome addition in the summer months. *Directions:* Rivière sur Tarn is located approximately 50 kilometers southeast of Rodez. Take D911 to Millau, turning off onto D9 towards the well-known canyons of Gorges du Tarn. After about 8 kilometers, turn right onto D107 and go through the town of Rivière sur Tarn, continuing towards the suburb of Les Salles. Look for a Chambres d'Hôtes sign indicating the Meljacs' driveway to the left.

LES SALLES
Hosts: Monsieur and Madame Jean Meljac
12640 Rivière sur Tarn, France
tel: 65.59.85.78
5 Rooms, all w/pvt. shower/sink;
  All share hallway WCs
Double: 180F, Triple: 230F
Table d'Hôte: 65F per person
Open all year
Very little English spoken
Region: Tarn

A cool oasis in this sometimes hot, dry climate, the Aboujoid's bed and breakfast offer a lovely azure pool which looks out over a spectacular view of the peaceful valley below. Young, friendly hosts Monsieur and Madame Aboujoid offer accommodation in their recently completed pool pavilion whose guest rooms open directly onto the pool's flagstone terrace. The Aboujoids' summer house is located a few steps away and has an inviting kitchen and dining room area where guests share breakfast, and if desired, Table d'Hôte dinners. This is an idyllic setting, perfect for travellers who would like to spend some time relaxing by the pool rather than rushing off on all day sightseeing excursions. Bedrooms are small and very simply furnished in a functional, basic style; each with private shower, sink and WC. *Directions:* Chez Aboujoid is actually loated in the small hamlet of Roquemaure. The nearest large town is St Sulpice which is located about 30 kilometers northeast of Toulouse. Take N88 in the direction of Albi for about 25 kilometers to St Sulpice. Turn left onto D630 in the directions of Montauban and continue to the village of Bessières, where you will turn right towards Mirepoix. Follow signs and arrows which direct you up a hill, then onto an unpaved country road to the Aboujoids' stone and tile-roofed house on the right.

LE PENDUT
Hosts: Monsieur and Madame Aboujoid
Roquemaure 81370 St Sulpice, France
tel: 63.41.90.07 or 61.84.10.23 (summer)
2 Rooms, both with prvt shower/WC
Single: 185F, Double: 200F, Triple: 230F
Table d'Hôte: 70F per person
Open June 1 through October 1
No English spoken
Region: Tarn

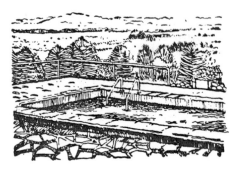

Mas Le Gramenier, an especially neat and tidy looking bed & breakfast, has been so meticulously redone that, although it dates from the 18th Century, at first we thought the building was new.   The exterior fairly gleams from the recent cleaning of the rosey-colored stone walls which are enhanced by freshly painted pale green shutters and doors.   The setting of this attractive farmhouse B&B is exceptionally appealing: seven acres of well-tended vineyards, vegetable gardens, fruit trees, and flower gardens delight the eye in every direction.   The decor within is not antique, but the furniture is simple and in keeping with a country mood.   One of the most outstanding aspects of Le Gramenier is its large swimming pool located in the back garden where one can rest after a day of sightseeing and soak in the beauty of the surrounding hills.   Reservations are only accepted with breakfast and dinner included in the room rate, but guests we spoke to said that the food is excellent. *Directions:* Roussillon is located 48 km northeast of Avignon.   From the N100, take the route north signposted "Roussillon" (the road is actually 149 but we did not see a sign).   Le Gramenier is about 1 km on the left side of the road.

MAS LE GRAMENIER
Host: Danielle & Laurence Haim
Roussillon
84220 Gordes, France
tel: 90 05 60 88
5 Rooms, all with private bath/WC
Double: 670F for two persons
rate includes breakfast & dinner
Table d'Hôte included in room rate
Credit cards: None accepted
Open from Easter to November
No English spoken
Region: Provence

A stay at La Bergerie is for travellers seeking inexpensive accommodation in an authentic French farm atmosphere. The facade of this three-storey farmhouse is softened by large easter lilies which grow under the front windows, and the small front lawn is dotted with hens and roosters strutting about looking for grain under a white lilac tree. We arrived on a Saturday afternoon, and Madame LeFrancois was busily preparing a dinner of fresh trout and farm vegetables for expected evening guests. She and her husband are an energetic couple who serve Ferme Auberge dinners on weekends, offering seating at five tables in their cosy dining room decorated by a large old fireplace, antiques and many flowers and plants. On weekdays, bed and breakfast guests can share family-style meals at the long table in Madame's farm kitchen. The two guest bedrooms are spacious and furnished with family antiques and home-like knicknacks. No English is spoken here, but Monsieur and Madame Le Francois (and their five children) offer an authentic slice of life and simple farm hospitality. *Directions:* St Arnoult is approximately 30 kilometers west of Rouen via D982. Just outside the town of Caudebec en Caux, still on D982 going towards Lillebonne, look for sign for a Ferme Auberge to the right. Continue following signs which will lead you to this three-story white farmhouse.

* LA BERGERIE
Hosts: Monsieur and Madame Le François
St Arnoult, 76490 Caudebec en Caux, France
tel: 35.56.75.84
2 Rooms, 1 with private bath, share WC
Single: 165F, Double: 165F, Triple: 250F
Ferme Auberge - Table d'Hôte: 60-70F per person
Open all year
No English spoken
Region: Normandy

At the edge of the small town of St Chartier, near the castle of 19th-century French novelist Georges Sand, Ralph Metz offers home-like bed and breakfast accommodation at Le Chalet. A medium-sized stone building dating from 1890, his house is shaped like an Alpine chalet; hence its unusual name. Monsieur Metz spent 22 years living and working overseas in Madagascar and Africa, and has filled his home with interesting artifacts from his life on the "dark continent". A fascinating collection of black and white photographs depicting African tribal life are displayed throughout his home and some especially lovely photos line the winding Italian staircase which leads up to the guest bedrooms. Rooms vary in size and decor, and contain basic, contemporary furnishings, with neutral colour schemes creating a somewhat masculine atmosphere. Informal breakfasts are shared in Monsieur's modern kitchen or enjoyed on the sunny back terrace. *Directions:* St Chartier is located approximately 30 kilometers southeast of Chateauroux. Travel south on D943 towards La Chatre, turning left onto D918 to St Chartier after about 25 kilometers. Once in the village of St Chartier, take D69 towards Verneuil and look for a Chambres d'Hôtes sign indicating a driveway on the left which enters the tree-shaded front yard of Le Chalet.

LE CHALET
Host: Monsieur Ralph Metz
Route de Verneuil
36400 St Chartier, France
tel: 54.31.05.76
4 Rooms, 2 w/pvt WC/shower others share
Single: 200F, Double: 230F
No Table d'Hôte
Open all year
Some English spoken
Region: Limousin

St Clar's market square is a pretty ensemble of stone arcaded buildings dating from the 17th century. This intimate "place" is a designated historic monument and is also the site of the old town hall: hence its name, Place de la Mairie. Nicole and Jean-Francois are an interesting, artistic young couple who live in a partially restored section of the buildings on the square and offer charming bed and breakfast accommodation to travellers. To reach their home, one enters through an arched stone doorway into a wide hallway, formerly horse stables, and ascends a stairway to the second floor. All the guest bedrooms are separate from the Cournots' living quarters. Madame has decorated the rooms in a charming, attractive style utilizing cheerful Laura Ashley wallpapers and bright, fresh colour schemes. Guests are welcome to relax in the Cournots' lovely salon which has exquisite 100-year-old gold leaf wallpaper still intact and a marble fireplace flanked by comfortable leather chairs and couch. Breakfast is served "en famille" in the cosy kitchen with a blue and white tile floor and rustic country antique furnishings. There is also a small kitchenette available for guests' use. *Directions:* St Clar is located about 40 km south of Agen. Take N21 towards Auch, turning left at Lectoure onto D7 to St Clar. In St Clar, follow signs for the Place de la Mairie.

CHEZ COURNOT
Hosts: Nicole and Jean-Francois Cournot
Place de la Mairie, 32380 St Clar, France
tel: 62.66.47.31
2 Rooms share separated WC and shower
Single: 115F, Double: 165F, Triple: 220F
Table d'Hôte: 85F per person
Reduced prices for 3 night reserved stays
Open all year
Some English spoken
Region: Tarn

The Gay family has recently constructed a wing of rooms for bed and breakfast guests which is a perfect stopping place for travellers seeking modern convenience over historical ambiance. Bedrooms are functional and attractive, all with shuttered French doors opening onto a covered outdoor hallway. The dimensions are small, but rooms are very comfortable, with great attention to detail such as soundproofing, good lighting, electrical plugs and spotless bathrooms. The Gays have also built a fully equipped kitchen at the end of the guest wing which is completely at guests' disposal. There is parking in the courtyard and a barbecue under an apricot tree, also for guest use. St Georges d'Orques is well known for the red wine produced in the region, and the Gays' home is located a bit out of town in a quiet setting of hills and vineyards. Monsieur and Madame have three sons who all speak English and are willing to help guests in any way they can. *Directions:* St Georges d'Orques is located approximately 8 kilometers west of Montpellier. Take N109 in the direction of Lodève, turning left at Juvignac onto D27e towards St Georges d'Orques. Once you are in the village, you will find Chambres d'Hôtes signs leading the way to the Gays' house on the edge of town.

RÉSIDENCE SÉRENIS
Hosts: Monsieur and Madame Gay
2, Chemin de Bouisson
34680 St Georges d'Orques, France
tel: 67.75.07.67
6 Rooms, all with private shower/WC
Single: 165F, Double: 200F, Triple: 240F
No Table d'Hôte, but kitchen available
Open all year
Good English spoken by sons
Region: West Provence

Set in the mystical marshlands of coastal Normandy, La Ferme de la Rivière is an imposing fortified farmhouse dating from the 16th century.   The main entry leads directly into an old tower and up a well-worn spiral staircase to the dining room. The friendly Marie family serve Ferme Auberge dinners as well as guest breakfasts in this warm, inviting room with its atmospheric stone floors, walk-in fireplace and country furniture.   Bedrooms are found upstairs, and most have enchanting views over the surrounding fields and marshes.   Two of the bedrooms are quite large, share a bath and WC, and can be rented as a suite. The two smaller bedrooms have an intimate charm all their own, and each has a private shower and WC.   All of the bedrooms are simply furnished, mostly in family antiques.   La Ferme de la Rivière is a rare find, offering charming, comfortable accommodations, delicious country cuisine, peaceful scenery, and a warm family welcome.   *Directions:* St Germain du Pert is located 28 kilometers west of Bayeux via N13.   Approximately 6 kilometers before Isigny sur Mer, turn left onto D199 which leads to St Germain du Pert. Continue through the very small village, then turn left onto D124 following signs for Ferme Auberge de la Rivière.   One kilometer later turn right at the Maries' gate which is marked with a sign.

LA FERME DE LA RIVIÈRE
Hosts: Paulette and Hervé Marie
14230 St Germain du Pert, France
tel: 31.22.72.92
4 Rooms, 2 share bath, separate WC,
* 2 Rooms with private bath/WC*
Single: 140F, Double: 180F, Triple: 230F
Table d'Hôte: 75F per person
Open Easter to October 30
Very little English spoken
Region: Normandy

The pretty old complex of La Croix de la Voulte is built of white, regional stone and dates from the 15th and 17th centuries.   All the guest bedrooms are found in an independent wing, and are newly renovated with much attention to detail.   A high level of comfort prevails; each WC is separate from the bathrooms, soft carpets cover the stone floors and luxurious bedding assures a good night's sleep.   Each room has a private entry and special character all its own.   The largest bedroom is very regal in style with a massive old stone fireplace, king-sized bed, old armoire and tapestry chairs.   Another is more feminine in decor, with rich rose-coloured wallpaper, matching curtains and complementary bedspreads. Low, beamed ceilings, light stone walls and lovely antique furniture add historical character to all the bedrooms.   The tranquil courtyard is a pleasant outdoor location to enjoy a leisurely breakfast, although guests may also elect to pamper themselves by being served in their room.   There is a refreshing pool available for guests' use on warm summer days. *Directions:* St Lambert des Levées is located about 3 kilometers west of Saumur on the north bank of the Loire.   Take D229 in the direction of St Martin de la Place, pass the Saumur train station and continue 3 kilometers until you see a Chambres d'Hôtes sign directing you to turn into a driveway on the right.

LA CROIX DE LA VOULTE
Hosts: Monsieur and Madame Minder
St Lambert des Levées, 49400 Saumur, France
tel: 41.38.46.66
4 Rooms, all with private bath/WC
Single: 270-390F, Double: 300-420F, Triple: 490F
Open all year
No Table d'Hôte
Fluent English spoken
Region: Loire Valley

La Pastourelle is a low, stone farmhouse whose construction is typical of the Brittany region. A pleasing construction is formed by grey stones of varying sizes mortared together in a seemingly haphazard manner: in fact it is easy to pick out one large boulder that was simply left in place and incorporated into the front wall of the house. The Lédés and their two young sons live in a separate wing of their pretty farmhouse, offering guests an independent entry, salon, dining room and five guest bedrooms. A charming, country ambiance is felt throughout, created by Madame's collection of lovely antiques and special touches such as wildflower bouquets. The bedrooms are spotlessly clean and tastefully decorated in dainty flower-print wallpaper, softly coloured carpets and crocheted bedspreads. Delicious Table d'Hôte dinners are served downstairs in the cosy dining room and often include local fish or grilled meats and regional specialties such as crepes or galettes. *Directions:* St Lormel is located approximately 66 kilometers northwest of Rennes, near the town of Plancoet. From Plancoet, travel north on D768 for 1 kilometer, then turn left onto D19 towards St Lormel. Before reaching the village, look for Chambres d'Hôtes signs indicating La Pastourelle which will lead to the Lédés' Breton farmhouse.

LA PASTOURELLE
Hostess: Madame Lédé
St Lormel, 22130 Plancoet, France
tel: 96.84.03.77
5 Rooms, all with private shower or bath/WC
Single: 180F, Double: 190F, Triple: 250F
Demi-pension: 145F per person
Open March through November
Very little English spoken
Region: Brittany

The Chateau de Vergières' magic begins as you approach by way of a tree-lined lane ending at the stately, three-story manor whose pastel facade is accented by white shuttered windows and heavy tiled roof.   The rather formal exterior belies the warmth of welcome one finds within.   For many years the chateau has been in the family of Marie-Andrée who has opened her heart and home to guests from all over the world.   She is ably assisted by her gracious husband, Jean Pincedé.   Inside as well as outside, the chateau reflects the patina of age displaying an ambiance of homey comfort.   Quality country antiques are everywhere, yet nothing is contrived, cutely "redone" or decorator perfect.   The dining room is especially outstanding with its beamed ceiling, fabulous antique armories, side board and long wooden table surrounded by French Provençal-style wooden chairs.   Be sure to plan ahead so you can have the fun of sharing a meal here with your fellow guests.   *Directions:* Vergières is located approximately 25 km southeast of Arles.   From St. Martin de Crau take D24 south toward La Dynamite and after 3 km watch for a small sign on the left side of the road to the Chateau de Vergières.   Turn left at the sign.   Continue for 4.3 km to the lane leading to the chateau.

CHATEAU DE VERGIÈRES
Hosts: Jean & Marie-Andrée Pincedé
Vergières, La Dynamite
13310 Saint Martin de Crau, France
tel: 90.47.17.16 fax: 90.47.38.30
6 Rooms, all with private bath/WC
Single: 800F, Double: 800F
Table d'Hôte: 250F per person
Credit cards: All major
Open March to October
Very good English Spoken
Region: Provence

Michel and Josette Garret are former prizewinning dairyfarmers who extend a warm, sincere welcome to their farm in the pastoral region north of Bordeaux. Their farmhouse is built in the typical regional style: long and low, of pretty warm-toned stone. They have completely renovated the interior; preserving the heavy beamed ceilings, exposing the light stone walls and adding cool tile floors and modern conveniences. Sharing an avid interest in local history and regional antiques, they have filled their home with lovely old pieces such as a huge Bordeaux armoire, a Louis XIV mantelpiece and a cherrywood grandfather clock. Bedrooms are prettily furnished and enhanced by French doors leading out to bucolic pasturelands. Since our last visit, an additional bedroom with private bathroom and WC has been added in a converted outbuilding. *Directions:* St Martin de Laye is located approximately 30 kilometers northeast of Bordeaux. Leave Bordeaux on N89 to Libourne, then take D910 to St Denis de Pile, where you will turn left over the bridge onto D22 towards Bonzac. Before arriving in St. Martin de Laye, take the turn marked "Gaudart Buisson". Turn left at the second driveway, and continue past the first farmhouse on the left to the Garrets' house at the end of the driveway.

CHEZ GARRET
Hosts: Michel and Josette Garret
St Martin de Laye
33910 St Denis de Pile
tel: 57.49.41.37   fax: 57.24.85.42
3 Rooms, all w/ pvt WC/bath or shower
Single: 120-180F, Double: 150-210F
Table d'Hôte: 70F per person
Open Easter through October 31
No English spoken
Region: Atlantic Coast

Monsieur and Madame Lawrence are an interesting, well-travelled couple who enjoy a healthy, outdoor lifestyle in the Provencal region.   Their lovely, golden-toned stone house is set on a tranquil hillside overlooking a breathtaking vista of vineyards and green hills.   Guests have a separate entrance through French doors off a shady terrace.   The guest bedroom has a mezzanine area for a third person, and is very tastefully decorated with a mixture of contemporary and antique furniture, Oriental rugs and a subtle colour scheme.   Some unusual and fascinating pieces such as a carved wooden chest from Monsieur and Madame's travels in Bali provide attractive accents to the room's decor.   A spotless and well-equipped bathroom completes the comfortable accommodation.   *Directions:* St Pantaléon is located approximately 40 kilometers east of Avignon.   Take N100 in the direction of Apt, turning left at the village of Coustellet towards Gordes.   After passing the hamlet of Les Imberts, turn right, following signs for St Pantaléon, until coming to a crossroads.   Continue straight through, avoiding the right turn into the village. Fifty metres farther, turn up the first small road on the left, and the first driveway on the right leads to the Lawrence home.

VILLA LA LEBRE
Hosts: Monsieur and Madame Lawrence
Pres de St Pantaléon
84220 Gordes
tel: 90.72.20.74
1 Room with private bath/WC
Single: 170F, Double: 185F, Triple: 250F
No Table d'Hôte
Open all year
Good English spoken
Region: Provence

Charles Henry de Valbray, affectionately known to family members as Charlie, has recently begun restoration and decoration of the Chateau Saint Paterne, in his family for over a century, but neglected and abandonned for the past 30 years. Henry IV used to rendezvous with his mistress here at Saint Paterne; his crest and the her initials can still be seen on the ceiling beam of one of the bedchambers. The magnificent bridal suite was Charlie's grandmother's room. It is large, overlooks the garden and in the morning the light plays on the yellow walls to cast a soft warm glow. The theme of the handsome Duck room relfects its name, and there is a single room for a child next to the bath. A ground floor room decorated in blue and white fabric and has a private entry and patio. All the rooms have direct dial phones and are individually decorated with family antiques and lovely fabrics. Guests are welcome to relax in the large salon where there is usually a cosy fire. The dining room is Charlie's pride and joy as he is the chef and delights in creating delicious dinners for his guests. Much work is still needed to bring the entire chateau back to the standard of luxury it once enjoyed, and Charlie has an endless list of enthusiastic plans. *Directions:* From Alençon, take D311 towards Mamers and Chartres. Look for sign to the Chateau de St Paterne before reaching the town of Mamers.

CHATEAU DU SAINT PATERNE
Host: Charles Henry de Valbray
72610 Saint Paterne
tel: 16.33.27.54.71
2 room/3 suites, all w/pvt baths
Double: 165F
Table d'Hôte: 200F per person
Closed January 15 to February 15
Good English spoken
Region: South Normandy

The Lot region can be almost unbearably hot and dry in the summer months, so the cool, inviting swimming-pool at Lou Castellou is truly a refreshing treat. The Bérangers are a warm, friendly couple who sincerely enjoy welcoming their guests and making them feel right at home. Their house is perched on a hill and is of recent construction, with equally modern decor and furnishings. Bedrooms are small but comfortable; furnished in a mix of antique and reproduction furniture and all offering pretty views over the surrounding countryside. Madame Béranger's home cooking is absolutely not to be missed: her Table d'Hôte dinners begin with a first course such as quiche, followed by a meat dish accompanied by two vegetables, a cheese course and dessert. The delicious cuisine is complemented by lively conversation and regional wines. In the true spirit of bed and breakfast, visitors have the feeling that they are family friends rather than hotel guests. *Directions:* St Pierre la Feuille is approximately 8 kilometers north of Cahors. Take N20 in the direction of Paris and just after the village of St Pierre la Feuille follow signs for Les Graves and Chambres à Louer (rooms to rent). A country lane and driveway on the left lead to the Bérangers' home.

LOU CASTELLOU
Hosts: Monsieur and Madame Béranger
Les Graves, St Pierre La Feuille
46090 Cahors
tel: 65.36.83.76
5 Rooms, 2 w/pvt WC/shower, others share
Single: 140F, Double: 165F, Triple: 208F
Table d'Hôte: 70F per person
Open all year
No English spoken
Region: Lot

The Chateau de Roussillon is an old fortified castle, partially in ruins, which is perched on a rock outcrop high above a deep valley. The existing castle and towers date from the 13th and 15th centuries, but were built on the remains of a far more ancient fortress. Madame Hourriez offers extremely romantic accommodation in the ancient tower chapel. The large guest room has a private bath and an independent entrance off the upper stone courtyard. A high stone vaulted ceiling and exposed stone walls lend a very medieval feeling to this spacious room furnished entirely in dark wood antiques, Oriental rugs and tapestry wall hangings. A comfortable double bed is found near a window set deep in the thick rock wall offering a spectacular view over the valley below. A cosy fireplace corner beckons in the evenings or on cool autumn afternoons. Madame brings breakfast every morning to the room or to the outdoor table and chairs in the courtyard garden. For longer stays, Madame Hourriez has an equally picturesque, fully-equipped apartment for up to six people. *Directions:* St Pierre la Feuille is located about 8 kilometers north of Cahors. Take N20 towards Paris and, once in the village of St Pierre, look for a sign pointing to the right for Chateau de Roussillon.

CHATEAU DE ROUSSILLON
Hostess: Madame Marcelle Hourriez
St Pierre la Feuille
46090 Cahors
tel: 65.36.87.05
1 Room with private shower/WC
Single: 320F, Double: 330F, Triple: 450F
No Table d'Hôte
Open all year
Very little English spoken
Region: Lot

The du Réau family has resided in this dramatic building since it was built in 1808. The current host is the very cultured, yet down-to-earth Jean du Réau who has taken great pleasure in renovating his family home so that he could offer bed and breakfast accommodation in this tranquil, authentic French country home setting. Monsieur du Réau offers breakfast in an intimate style in his country kitchen, seated at a long wooden table facing an old stone fireplace and copper pots filled with graceful yellow wildflowers.   The epitome of the French country gentleman, Monsieur sports a handlebar moustache and is most often found smoking his aromatic pipe.   He was actually born in one of the beds upstairs, in the same room where one can admire a lovely portrait of his mother, painted when she was five years old. All of the bedrooms have been freshly renovated with tasteful wallpapers and furnished with impressive family antiques, mostly from the Empire period.   This is a very special bed and breakfast where guests may experience a deeply engrained, authentic sense of the past, complete with gracious host and comfortable surroundings. *Directions:* St Rémy la Varenne is located about 14 kilometers east of Angers on the Loire's south bank.   Take D952 to the village of St Rémy la Varenne where Chambres d'Hôtes signs lead the way to Monsieur du Réau's driveway.

CHATEAU DES GRANGES
Host: Monsieur Jean du Réau
Bourg, 49250 St Rémy la Varenne
tel: 41.57.02.13
3 Rooms, all with shower/basin, share one WC
Single: 240F, Double: 350F
No Table d'Hôte
Open all year; winter by reservation only
Some English spoken
Region: Loire Valley

Each summer Martin and Beth Silvester left the rain and chill of their native England to holiday in France. On each visit they looked for a place to retire and finally found the perfect spot, a handsome stone manorhouse - bright and cheerful inside with tall windows (framed in light green shutters) letting in the sun. After extensive renovations, they have opened one wing of their home into a bed and breakfast. A fabulous old wooden spiral staircase (dating back to the 1700's) winds up to three bedrooms which, although not "decorator perfect" are homey and comfortable. Ask for the blue bedroom at the top of the stairs: it is the most attractive with a lovely antique wooden "sleigh" bed, antique dresser, rich planked wooden floors, a modern bathroom with skylight and French casement windows overlooking the terrace. In the front of the manor is a large swimming pool, a welcome respite for a hot day after sightseeing. Even if you speak French, it might be a welcome relief to slip back into English again for a few days and not have to tax your vocabulary skills. *Directions:* St Romain is located 95 km northeast of Bordeaux. Take the D2 east from Chalais. Just before Aubeterre, when the road forks, turn left on D10 (signposted Montmoreau). Manoir de la Sauzade is about 1 km on the left side of the road.

LA SAUZADE
Hosts: Martin & Beth Silvester
16210 St Romain, France
tel: 45.98.63.93
3 Rooms, all with private bath/WC
Double: 300F
No Table d'Hôte
Credit cards: None
Open Easter to October
Fluent English spoken
Region: Atlantic Coast

The Arredondo family's old stone farmhouse lies in a hilly, forested region 20 kilometers north of the medieval town of Carcassonne. Monsieur and Madame and their two grown sons raise veal, sheep, fowl, cows and horses, as well as plenty of friendly tabby cats. The Arredondos offer a true country bed and breakfast experience, complete with guided horseback tours of the region and Table d'Hôte dinners. Their own farm products are featured at meals, which might include homemade pates and sausage followed by a chicken dish, garden vegetables and salad, local cheese, and dessert. The dining room is rustic and intimate, with a stairway at the far end leading up to the guest bedrooms. Located in a renovated attic, the rooms are small but very fresh and clean. Madame Arredondo has decorated each room individually with charming flower print and lace curtains, beds and night tables. *Directions:* Saissac is located southeast of Toulouse and 20 kilometers north of Carcassonne. Leave Carcassonne on N113 in the direction of Castelnaudary. After about 7 kilometers, turn right onto D629 and continue through the village of Montolieu, following signs for Saissac and Revel. Go through the village of Saissac and look for a Chambres d'Hôtes sign which directs to the right and up a hill. Leave town and travel about 3 kilometers on a country road looking for a Chambres d'Hôtes sign directing to their driveway on the left.

DOMAINE DE L'ALBEJOT
Hosts: Monsieur and Madame Arredondo
11310 Saissac, France
tel: 68.24.44.03
5 Rooms, 2 w/pvt WC/bath, others share
Single: 140-160F, Double: 200-260F
Table d'Hôte: 70F per person
Open all year
Very little English, fluent Spanish
Region: Languedoc-Roussillon

The flower-filled medieval village of Salers is perched on a high point in the mountainous region of central France. Officially classified as one of the prettiest villages in France, it is a picturesque jumble of quaint, cottage-style houses and shops, all built from regional grey stone and with slate roofs. Young hosts Claudine and Philippe Prudent offer travellers comfortable and practical accommodation in a separate wing of their historic house. Bedrooms are all similar in decor, featuring country-style beds, tables and chairs and small alcoves with shower, wash-basin and WC. Exposed ceiling beams and dormer windows add character to the functional rooms. Guest quarters are accessed through a peaceful green garden which has a magnificent view over the surrounding hills and valleys. Breakfast in served here in this tranquil, natural setting or, if preferred, in guest bedrooms. *Directions:* Salers is located approximately 35 kilometers north of Aurillac. Take D922 north towards Mauriac on a winding, hilly road, turning right onto D680 towards Salers. Travel through the village on narrow cobblestone streets all the way to the central square. Turn left down the rue des Nobles and look for a Chambres d'Hôtes sign marking the Prudents' house.

CHEZ PRUDENT
Hosts: Claudine and Philippe Prudent
Rue des Nobles
15410 Salers, France
Tel: 71.40.75.36
6 Rooms, all with private shower/WC
Single: 181F, Double: 202F, Triple: 233F
No Table d'Hôte
Open all year
Some English spoken
Region: Auvergne

A large, ivy-covered house on a hill overlooking peaceful pasturelands is the setting for the Domaine des Hautes Cimes bed and breakfast.　The Prunet family live in a house next door, thus offering completely private guest accommodation. Breakfast is usually served in the light, airy dining room of the guest house, furnished in country antiques with inviting details such as an old stone fireplace and beamed ceiling.　The guest house also has an inviting salon with a television and comfortable seating.　One bedroom is filled with family antiques, but most have simple, country-style pine furniture and provide basic comforts. *Directions:* La Salesse is located approximately 35 kilometers southeast of Aurillac.　Scenic winding roads are the only way to reach this lovely, yet isolated spot.　Leave Aurillac in the direction of Rodez, turning off after 4 kilometers, just after Arpajon sur Cère towards Vezac and Carlat.　At the town of Raulhac, turn left onto D990 and after about 3 kilometers turn right onto small country road towards Brommes. At the next intersection, turn left on D79 towards Douzalbats and Frons.　Less than 1 kilometer later, turn right up a TINY lane which winds up to La Salesse.　As you enter the hamlet, the Prunets' gate is straight ahead, while the road veers to the left and into the village.

DOMAINE DES HAUTES CIMES
Hosts: Monsieur and Madame Prunet
La Salesse, 12600 Mur de Barrez, France
Tel: 65.66.14.27
5 Rooms, all w/bath or shower, 1 w/private WC
Single: 100F, Double: 120F, Triple: 135F
No Table d'Hôte
Open all year
No English spoken
Region: Auvergne

Although only about 20 years old, Aguzan, a pretty tiled roof home almost entirely laced with ivy, exudes an aura of agelessness.   The living room with large fireplace, beamed ceiling and family antiques, reflects a sophisticated yet very comfortable, home-like ambiance.   There are four bedrooms for guests.   Our favorites were the two upstairs: One is a very prettily decorated single room overlooking the garden, the other a double, attractively decorated with red and white wall paper and coordinating fabric on the bed.   Although the rooms have a wash basin in the room, none has a private bathroom.   One of the best features of the house is the park-like rear garden.   The owners, M and Mme Langer, do not speak English, but are gracious hosts and their home has an ambiance of spaciousness and refinement. *Directions:* located 9km northeast of La Rochelle.   Once in La Rochelle, take the D9 toward Puilboreau-Luçon (street Maaius-la Croix).   After the village St Xandre, take the road on the right toward La Sauzaie.   In La Sauzaie go in the direction of Usseau, then the first road on the right (street du Chateau).   The second lane to your left leads to Aguzan.

AGUZAN
Host: Annick Langer
rue du Chateau, La Sauzaie
17138 Saint Xandre, France
tel: 46.37.22.65
4 Rooms, none with private bath/WC
Single: 190F, Double: 240F
No Table d'Hôte
Credit cards: None
Open all year
No English spoken
Region: Atlantic Coast

Le Prieuré is a favourite on our list of bed and breakfasts, offering a warm welcome in a tranquil, appealing setting.   This 15th-century cottage recalls the days of Joan of Arc with its low beamed ceilings, walk-in fireplaces and old stone walls. Madame Caré is a motherly hostess who obviously takes great pleasure in welcoming guests to her charming, ivy-covered home.   Her well-tended garden provides fresh flower bouquets throughout her rooms which are furnished in highly polished family antiques.   Bedrooms are comfortable and extremely romantic with exposed stone walls, old fireplaces and charming stone window seats.   Small paned, lead-glass windows look out over the peaceful courtyard and "secret" garden. A hidden path leads up to this green haven where one is tempted to spend a lazy afternoon with book in hand or simply listening to the occasional birdsong.   It is the fortunate traveller indeed who has the chance to stay at this enchanting bed and breakfast.   *Directions:* Savonnières is located about 11 kilometers west of Tours on the south bank of the Loire via D7 in the direction of Villandry.   Once in the village of Savonnières look for Chambres d'Hôtes signs which lead to Madame Caré's driveway.

LE PRIEURÉ
Hostess: Madame Lucette Caré
10, rue Chaude
Savonnières, France
37510 Joué les Tours
tel: 47.50.03.26
1 2-bedroom Suite with one bath/WC
Single 220F, Double 275F, Triple 355F
No Table d'Hôte
Open all year
No English spoken
Region: Loire Valley

The Lethuilliers built their Norman dream house seven years ago near the picturesque port town of Fécamp and the spectacular cliffs of Étretat. The entire house is furnished in lovely antiques, complemented by pretty flowered wallpapers, Oriental rugs and fresh flower arrangements. Madame Lethuillier proudly displays her collections of brass and copper artifacts on the living room mantel, as well as a fine collection of old plates that once belonged to her grandmother. Madame Lethuillier is a talented seamstress, and her artistic flair is evident in every room, creating a pleasing feeling of home-like elegance. Breakfast can be enjoyed either in the inviting salon (complete with tabby cat curled up on a chair cushion) or, weather permitting, on the terrace overlooking the front garden and goldfish pond. The Lethuillers do not speak English, but their British daughter-in-law lives nearby and is happy to stop by to help with any communication difficulties. *Directions:* Senneville is located approximately 45 kilometers northeast of Le Havre via D940 changing to D925 after Fécamp: on D925 the route is well-marked by signs for Chambres d'Hôtes. Follow a country lane bordered by wildflowers, turning right at a small sign for Val de la Mer.

CHEZ LETHUILLIER
Hosts: Mireille Lethuillier
Val de la Mer, Senneville sur Fécamp
76400 Fecamp, France
tel: 35.28.41.93
3 Rooms, 1 with private WC/shower
Single: 220F, Double: 240F, Triple: 310F
No Table d'Hôte
Open all year
No English spoken
Region: Normandy

Located in the heart of the Burgundy wine region, Maryse and Philippe Viardot's charming home is an ideal base from which to explore the surrounding countryside and sample the renowned local wines. Although their 200-year-old house is found in a small village, it remains a quiet haven; set back from the street and bordered by a peaceful garden. Madame is an energetic hostess with a real flair for decoration who has managed to capture just the right blend of contemporary design and old-fashioned ambiance in her home and guest rooms. Bedrooms are highly tasteful combinations of soft colour schemes, pretty country antiques and carefully-chosen artwork. Fresh flowers and plants personalize the attractive rooms, making guests feel right at home. Warm, sunny mornings mean breakfast in the garden, while in cooler weather it is served in the shelter of a pleasant, glass-enclosed veranda. *Directions:* Senozan is located approximately 15 kilometers north of Macon. Take N6 towards Tournus, turning off after 10 kilometers following signs for Senozan. Just after entering the village, look for a small stone church on the right. Across the street you will see a stone entryway, set back between two houses, and marked with a Chambres d'Hôtes sign. Turn left and drive through this portal to the end of the driveway, passing the houses closest to the road.

CHEZ VIARDOT
Hosts: Maryse and Philippe Viardot
Rue du Chateau
Le Bourg Senozan 71260, France
tel: 85.36.00.96
6 Rooms, 4 w/private bath, 3 share 1 bath/WC
Single: 180F, Double: 250F, Triple: 300F
No Table d'Hôte
Open all year
Very little English spoken
Region: Burgundy

The Jezequel family offers old-fashioned hospitality and delicious farm-fresh meals at the quaint Ferme Auberge de Sepvret.   Their 300-year-old home is covered with ivy and surrounded by a pretty, flower-filled garden.   Farm inn meals are served in the intimate and home-like dining room furnished with round wooden tables adorned with bouquets of fresh flowers and a cheerful selection of tablecloths. Traditional home-cooked fare features regional specialties such as "farci poitevin", a type of souffle made from garden greens (spinach, cabbage, parsley and sorrel), eggs, sour cream and spices.   Simple country charm is felt throughout the house and in the guest bedrooms which are furnished with brass beds, old armoires and flowered wallpapers.   Large windows open out to the back garden, letting in plenty of light and fresh air.   Days usually begin with a romantic and peaceful breakfast enjoyed outdoors at a table set under the trees. *Directions:* Sepvret is located about 45 kilometers southwest of Poitiers.   Take N10 towards Angoulême for 2 kilometers, then turn off onto N11 (which later becomes D150) and travel in the direction of Niort, la Rochelle and Saintes.   Turn right after about 40 kilometers onto D108 to Sepvret.   Once in the village, follow signs for Chambres d'Hôtes and Ferme Auberge which lead to the Jezequels' home.

FERME AUBERGE DE SEPVRET
Hosts: Francoise and Claude Jezequel
Sepvret, 79120 Lezay, France
tel: 49.07.33.73
4 Rooms, all w/pvt WC/shower or bath
Single: 120F, Double: 140F, Triple: 180F
Table d'Hôte: 60F per person
Open May to September
Very little English spoken
Region: Atlantic Coast

Emile and Gilberte Moynier are wonderfully warm and solicitous hosts. Their 17th-century manor house is set back from the main road behind trees framing a magical view of the green valley and distant mountain peaks. Gilberte has decorated each of the guest bedrooms differently, combining classic country charm with her own personal artistic style. Les Hirondelles (The Nightengales) has dainly, mauve-flowered curtains and matching bedspreads on lovely old wooden beds complemented by a matching armoire, while Les Tilleuls (The Lime Trees) is bright and fresh with hindpainted furniture and tall windows looking out over the front garden. A separate dining room/kitchen/lounge area is available for guests' use. Formerly a sheep stall, it now has a cozy ambiance created by low, vaulted ceilings and walls of exposed stone sheltering rustic country antiques and a cheerful fire blazing in the hearth. *Directions:* Serres is located approximately 34 km southwest of Gap. Take D994 past Veynes to the town of Aspres sur Bruech. Leave town on N75 going south towards Nice. About 6 km later, before the village of Serres, look for signs for L'Alpillonne and a sign advertising Chambres d'Hôtes; English spoken. The Moyniers' driveway is on the left and is easy to miss.

L'ALPILLONNE
Hosts: Emile and Gilberte Moynier
La Plaine de Sigottier
Serres 05700 Sigottier, France
tel: 92.67.08.98
3 Rooms, 1 w/private shower/WC, 2 share 1 bath/WC
Single: 150F, Double: 240F, Triple: 300F
Table d'Hôte: 70F per person
  Demi-pension: 170 per person
Open June 15 to September 30
Good English spoken
Region: Maritime Alps

Located in the heart of the Brittany countryside, the Lolliers' farm is in a peaceful, scenic setting of wooded hills, pastures and streams. There is an inviting garden and front terrace leading up to this typically Breton, grey and white stone farmhouse. Inside, the attic guest rooms are simple yet charming, with sloping roofs and skylight windows. Two flights of a stairway which becomes narrow and steep at the top must be negotiated to arrive at the small sitting area on the top-floor landing which leads to the bedrooms. Furnishings are contemporary and tasteful, and the shared bathroom has fresh pine panelling. In the mornings, a copious breakfast is served downstairs in the cosy dining room: Madame Lollier's hot crepes, coffee cakes, homemade preserves, fruit juice, and coffee, tea or hot chocolate provide a delicious way to start the day. A old wooden chest is filled with a plate collection, while pretty wood floors, a country armoire, grandfather clock and dried flower arrangements combine to create a very inviting and welcoming ambiance. *Directions:* Spézet is located approximately 41 kilometers northeast of Quimper. Take D15 towards Gourin, turning left onto D82 towards Spézet after about 32 kilometers. Just after entering Spézet, turn right just before a restaurant, La Cremaillerie. Continue following Chambres d'Hôtes signs for about 1.5 kilometers to the Lollier's two-storey house on the right.

PENDREIGNE
Hosts: Monsieur and Madame Lollier
29540 Spézet, France
tel: 98.93.80.32
2 Rooms, share bath and WC
Single: 120F, Double: 160F
No Table d'Hôte
Open all year
No English spoken
Region: Brittany

The Juin-Paquiers' 19th-century manor house is found in a lovely countryside setting of rolling hills, forests and pasturelands. Their property encompasses 13 acres of lakes, fields and stately oak trees, offering inexhaustible opportunities for long, peaceful walks. The interior of their gracious home offers an inviting glimpse back into the past, as floors are original tile or hardwood and furnishings are all lovely family antiques. Monique has added some feminine touches such as flower-print curtains and bedspreads and lace-trimmed pillowslips to the guest bedrooms, which brighten the sometimes stark decor. Bathrooms are adequate and contain thoughtful details such as heart-shaped soaps and fluffy towels. Monique and Jean are personable and friendly hosts who have lived most of their lives in Paris but now prefer the more relaxed and informal country life. They are extremely helpful and welcoming and are happy to help guests plan sightseeing excursions in the area. *Directions:* Thivalière is located approximately 30 kilometres northeast of Montluçon. Take D94 to Cosne d'Allier, going through town and continuing north on D16 in the direction of Cerilly. After about 4 kilometres, look for a Chambres d'Hôtes sign directing you to turn left down a pretty country lane. Follow arrows which lead to the Juin-Paquiers' country home.

CHEZ JUIN-PAQUIER
Hosts: Monique and Jean Juin-Paquier
Thivalière
Louroux Bourbonnais, 03350 Cerilly, France
tel: 70.07.54.03
5 Rooms, 3 with private bath
Single: 120-150F, Double: 220-245F
No Table d'Hôte
Open all year
No English spoken
Region: Berry

If you are looking for a bed and breakfast convenient to Paris and close to Fontainbleau, Vivescence, located in the pretty village of Thomery, makes a good choice.   The home, ideally located on the main square opposite the church, looks like most of its neighbors from the front.   However, a surprise awaits: the back of the house opens up onto an expansive park.   The well-tended lawn sweeps to a rim of flowers and beautiful trees: although it cannot compete with Fontainbleau, for a private home, the garden is truly outstanding.   Viviescence is also a health center, and hosts various groups and fitness seminars.   There are some guest rooms available in the annex where the conferences are held, but these do not have much personality.   Ask for one of the large bedrooms in the main house overlooking the garden.   An added bonus is a heated indoor swimming pool which opens onto its own pretty walled garden.   In addition, there is a sauna that guests may use. *Directions:* Thomery is located 7 km east of Fontainbleau.   From Fontainbleau Chateau, take the N6 east for approximately 4 km and then turn left on the D301 (signposted Champagne, Thomery) and follow the signs to Thomery centre. Vivescence is located on the main square accross the street from the church.

VIVESCENCE
Host: Brigitte Stacke
9, Place Greffulhe
77810 Thomery, France
tel: 1.60.96.43.96 fax: 1.60.96.41.13
9 Rooms, 9 with private bath/WC
Single: 300F, Double: 350F, Triple: 400F
Table d'Hôte: 100F per person
Credit cards: None
Open all year except Christmas
Fluent English spoken
Region: Ile de France

The Juchereaus offer home-like accommodation in their rustic farmhouse, located on the edge of the scenic Marais de Poitevin. The Marais is a lush and verdant marshland full of canals and waterways where picturesque flat boats reminiscent of Venetian gondolas are used for transportation. The Juchereaus' charming guest bedrooms are decorated with matching curtains and bedspreads and furnished with a harmonious mix of antiques and reproductions. These young hosts are friendly and solicitous of their guests, and offer Table d'Hôte dinners featuring fresh home cooking. Their informal, familial dining room has exposed stone walls and is furnished in a rustic style with ladder-backed chairs and a country chest filled with faience plates. On warm mornings, the sunny, peaceful back garden is a pleasant place to breakfast or simply give in to the beckoning lawn chairs. *Directions:* Le Thou is located approximately 18 kilometres east of La Rochelle. Take D939 towards Surgeres for about 15 kilometres, then turn right onto D5 in the direction of Rochefort. Two kilometres later turn left towards Le Thou. Follow signs to the small settlement of Maisonneuve and then look for a Chambres d'Hôtes sign marking the Juchereaus' green shuttered farmhouse.

CHEZ JUCHEREAU
Hosts: Monsieur and Madame Juchereau
11, rue Maisonette du Bois
Maisonneuve, Le Thou, France
17290 Aigrefeuille
tel: 46.35.72.91
4 Rooms, all w/pvt shower/share 2 hall WCs
Single: 130F, Double: 160F, Triple: 220F
Table d'Hôte: 60F per person
Open all year
Very little English spoken
Region: Atlantic Coast

Located near the historical ruins of a fortified castle, Le Queffiou is an attractive, turn-of-the-century house with a large garden. Refined hostess Madame Sadoc offers a very warm welcome, along with highly comfortable accommodation including spotless, luxurious bathrooms supplied with big fluffy towels and sweet-smelling soap. The bedrooms are feminine and traditionally French in their decor and furnishings except for one which is a complete departure in style: high-tech modern. A solicitous hostess, Madame Sadoc pays great attention to detail and is a gourmet cook. Breakfasts are copious: the usual French bread and strong coffee, tea or chocolate accompanied by hot, buttery croissants, coffee cake and fresh fruit. Table d'Hôte dinners at Le Queffiou are enjoyable and delicious, served with style in the intimate dining room. *Directions:* Tonquédec is located approximately 25 kilometres northwest of Guingamp. Travelling on D767 from Guingamp, turn onto D31 just after Cavan towards Tonquédec. Go through the village, following signs for the Chateau de Tonquédec. After passing the chateau, there is a Chambres d'Hôtes sign directing you to turn left into the Sadocs' driveway.

LE QUEFFIOU
Hostess: Odette Sadoc
Route du Chateau
Tonquédec 22140, France
tel: 96.35.84.50
5 Rooms, all with private bath or shower/WC
Double: 300-330F
Table d'Hôte: 120F per person
Open all year
Very little English spoken
Region: Brittany

Manoir de l'Hormette is a beautiful farmhouse in Aignerville. The garden setting is very restful, protected and enclosed by the stone walls. The grounds are meticulous, beautifully groomed and planted. Inside, the warmth of the family and their welcome is evident in the decor and their thoughtful touches. A loft bedroom with sitting room below is found on the first floor. The second floor of the main house offers a double room, a twin room, and a small single room with sleigh bed. An apartment in the separate cottage has its own living room, darling wood table, tv, single day bed in living room, twin bedded room, double room and one bath. The kitchen is a masterpiece and Monsieur's collection of homemade vinegars sit above the window ledge. The dining room is very handsome, and outside tables await a sunny morning for a wonderful breakfast repast. *Directions:* Located 15 kilometers northwest of Bayeux off the N13. Travelling the N13 from Bayeux to Isigny, take the "Aignerville" exit to the left. Six hundred meters from the highway, at the first cross-road, turn left. The Manoir is 150 meters on the right at the second white fence.

MANOIR DE L'HORMETTE
Hosts: Monsieur & Madame Yves Corpet
Aignerville
14710 Trévières
tel: 31.22.51.79   fax: 31.22.75.99
3 Rooms, 2 Cottages/duplex with kitchen, 1 Studio
Double: 490-940F
Table d'Hôte: 220F per person
Credit cards: VS, MC
Open End of March to end of December
Some English spoken
Region: Normandy

The Rocagels' contemporary chalet is found on a hillside overlooking a lovely Alpine panorama. Their pretty home was recently built, and has charming rustic touches such as flower-filled windowboxes and a light-toned wood balcony and shutters. Inside, home-like knicknacks and contemporary decor create an unsophisticated, informal atmosphere. Guest bedrooms have independent entries, modern furnishings and bright colour schemes. Madame Rocagel is a very fastidious hostess who keeps her home spotlessly clean and takes a personal interest in her guests, offering a wealth of information on local sights and activities. She is rightfully proud of her culinary skills and enjoys offering Table d'Hôte dinners featuring regional specialties. We dined on a savoury meal of sausage and potatoes with cheese and onions, accompanied by green salad, local cheeses and a strawberry tart. *Directions:* Trevignin is located approximately 10 kilometres east of Aix les Bains. Leave Aix crossing the overpass above the freeway to the village of Mouxy on the Route du Revard. At Mouxy, turn left onto D913, still following Route du Revard. Continue past Trevignin and turn left towards St Victor at an intersection marked by a large stone cross. The Rocagels' two-storey home is the first house on the left.

LA REVARDIÈRE
Hosts: Monsieur and Madame Rocagel
Hameau de St Victor
Trevignin 73100 Aix-les-Bains, France
tel: 79.61.59.12
3 Rooms, 1 w/private bath/WC, 2 share bath/WC
Single: 170-200F, Double: 256-290F, Triple: 342F
Table d'Hôte: 85-175F per person
Open all year
No English spoken
Region: French Alps

The Le Rouzics' attractive, contemporary house is situated on the picturesque Trinité inlet overlooking peaceful sailboats moored between gray rock cliffs and dark green pines. Monsieur and Madame are a young couple who have recently converted part of their home into comfortable bed and breakfast accommodation with scenic views over the water and surrounding countryside. The bedrooms are sparkling clean and furnished in a tasteful, modern style with fresh pine wood or wallpapered walls. The Le Rouzics invite guests to make themselves at home and enjoy the television and stereo in the casual salon. An adjoining glassed-in veranda with a glorious southern exposure is a relaxing spot to enjoy breakfast above the pretty inlet. Early-morning guests are even treated to the sight of playful wild rabbits who inhabit the surrounding fields and hedgerows. *Directions:* La Trinité sur Mer and the village of Le Latz are located approximately 26 kilometres west of Vannes. Take N165 to Auray, then D28 towards Locmariaquer and La Trinité sur Mer. After crossing the Pont (bridge) de Kerisper, take the first right and continue straight ahead, following signs for Le Chateau du Lac. Take the dirt road that circles the chateau to the left, following it around to the right, and look for arrows directing you to Chambres d'Hôtes. The Le Rouzics' driveway and white Breton-style house will be on the right.

LA MAISON DU LATZ
Host: Nicole Le Rouzic
Le Latz, 56470 La Trinité sur Mer, France
tel: 97.55.80.91
4 Rooms, all with private bath/WC
Double: 240-270F, Triple: 320-400F
Table d'Hôte: 80F per person
Open all year
Very little English spoken
Region: Brittany

A small, picturesque village in the foothills of the French Alps is the scenic setting for Monique and Bernard Bornens' restored farmhouse. Their windows look out over peaceful rolling hills dotted with trees and wildflowers and caressed by sweet-smelling country air. The Bornens' house is home-like and modest, and the welcome they offer is warm and sincere. Table d'Hôte dinners are a wonderful opportunity to spend time with the Bornens and their teenage children, and are enjoyed in the light, airy dining/sitting room furnished in pretty wood antiques and reproductions. Bedrooms are similarly furnished, and are very clean and comfortable. Decor is pleasing; subtly colored curtains and wallpapers and crocheted bedspreads. Bathroom facilities are shared but very up-to-date and well-equipped, with obvious care taken during renovation to install a high level of modern comfort. *Directions:* Usinens is located approximately 50 kilometres southwest of Geneva. From autoroute A40 take the Francy Annecy exit and follow signs for Seyssel. Before arriving at Seyssel, look for a turnoff to the right for Usinens. Climb a pretty country road for about 2 kilometres, and once in the village of Usinens, take the first right turn. Look for a Chambres d'Hôtes sign which directs to the right through an old stone arch to the Bornens' driveway.

CHEZ BORNENS
Hosts: Monique and Bernard Bornens
Le Chef Lieu, 74910 Usinens, France
tel: 50.77.90.08
3 Rooms, share 1 shower and 1 bath
Single: 70F, Double: 95-125F, Triple: 157F
Table d'Hôte: 53F per person
Open all year
No English spoken
Region: Rhône/Alps

The ancient Roman town of Vaison la Romaine is found in a hilly, wooded setting in northern Provence. Just outside of town on a high point affording panoramic views of the surrounding mountains and plains, the Delesses' 150-year-old stone house offers a refined haven for travellers. The guest bedroom is a bit removed from the main part of the house, well soundproofed by thick old stone walls and accessible from an independent entrance. French doors lead out to an intimate terrace overlooking a restful view of fields and distant hills. The room is tastefully decorated and very comfortable, with a writing table and bookcase stocked for guest enjoyment. Monsieur and Madame are both teachers, and specialize in French and English respectively, so communication with their English-speaking guests is no problem, and convivial breakfasts are enjoyed together in their cosy beamed breakfast room or outside in the tranquil front courtyard. A pool has been added since our visit. *Directions:* Vaison la Romaine is located about 18 kilometres north of Carpentras via D938. If coming from Avignon, follow signs to Orange, and then for Vaison la Romaine. Upon entering the town, turn left at the first trafficlight, then take the first left at the high school, then right, then left again. The Delesses' driveway is on the right and is marked with a Chambres d'Hôtes sign.

CHEZ DELESSE
Hosts: Francois and Claude Delesse
Chemin de l'Ioou
Le Brusquet, 84110 Vaison la Romaine, France
tel: 90.36.38.38
1 Room with private bath
Single: 180F, Double: 200F, Triple: 250F
No Table d'Hôte
Open all year
Very good English spoken
Region: Provence

The *Haute Ville* of Vaison-la-Romaine, an unspoiled fortified village rising steeply from the banks of the L'Ouveze River, has a superb bed and breakfast, owned by the Verdier family. Jean, an architect, and Aude, his pretty wife, moved from Paris to the ancient walled city of Vaison-La-Romaine in 1975. They worked together to transform the ruins of what was once a part of the bishop's palace, into a gracious home for themselves and their three sons. Three of the bedrooms are kept for bed and breakfast guests who also have a private entrance onto the street and an exclusive lounge. Of the guest rooms, my favorites were the twin bedded rooms which have more of an antique ambiance then the double bedded room which has a bit of an art deco feel. Aude serves breakfast on an enticing terrace snuggled amongst the rooftops, or when the weather is chilly, in the family dining room. Although Aude and Jean speak only a smattering of high school English, their absolutely genuine warmth will guarantee a very special stay. *Directions:* Vaison la Romaine is located 45 km northeast of Avignon. When you reach the town of Vaison la Romaine, cross the river and climb the narrow road to the Ville Médievalé. The L'Éveché on the right side of the main street, Rue de l'Éveché.

L'ÉVÊCHÉ
Hosts: Aude & Jean Loup Verdier
Rue de l'Évêché, Ville Médievalé
84110 Vaison la Romaine
tel: 90.36.13.46   fax: 90.36.32.43
3 Rooms, all with private bath/WC
Single: 250-290F, Double: 290-330F, Triple: 400-450F
No Table d'Hôte
Credit cards: None
Open January to December
Very little English spoken
Region: Provence

In French, La Maison aux Volets Bleus means The House of the Blue Shutters: indeed, the bright cobalt shutters of the Marets' charming home can be seen from far below the hilltop town of Venasque.   Follow a winding road up from the plains to this ancient town which is now a haven for painters and art lovers.   An old stone archway leads to the Marets' doll-like walled garden and their picturesque home filled with colorful dried flower bouquets hanging from every available rafter. Each bedroom is unique and decorated with Martine Maret's artistic flair in harmonious colours, Provençal prints, and simple, attractive furnishings.   Martine and her husband Jerome are an energetic young couple with many talents who enjoy welcoming guests into their home and to their table.   Reserve well in advance in order to enjoy a stay with the Marets at the Maison aux Volets Bleus. *Directions:* Venasque is located approximately 8 kilometres southeast of Carpentras via D4 towards Apt.   Look for the turnoff marked Venasque to the right up a hill. Continue to the fountain square (Place de la Fontaine) and look for a Chambres d'Hôtes sign to the left indicating the arched entry to the Marets' home.

LA MAISON AUX VOLETS BLEUS
Hosts: Martine and Jerome Maret
Place des Bouviers
Le Village, 84210 Venasque, France
tel: 90.66.03.04
6 Rooms, all with private bath or shower/WC
Single: 230F, Double: 260-330F, Triple: 360-430F
Table d'Hôte: 100F per person
Open March 15 through November 11
Good English spoken
Region: Provence

The imposing, red-brick Chateau de Jallanges is skilfully looked after by young Stéphane Balin and his fiancée. A fortified castle stood on this site in the 1200s, and the current castle built in 1480 reflects the beginning of the Renaissance period in French history. It is easy to take a mental journey back in time while enjoying a house specialty aperitif on the back terrace which overlooks a green lawn shaded by three stately old cedar trees. The Balins strive to maintain a relaxing, aristocratic ambiance and to offer their guests a chance to experience an authentic taste of life in a French Renaissance castle. Breakfasts are gourmet delights which include two kinds of fresh, homemade pastries and natural fruit juices in addition to the usual breakfast fare. The guest suites each have two small, intimate bedrooms furnished with a delicate feminine touch. One room features a romantic brass bed covered with a pretty lace bedspread. Also at guests' disposal is an elegant wood-panelled salon and a billiard room. Another wing of the castle is open to the public for tours and tastings of local wines. *Directions:* Vernou sur Brenne is located approximately 12 kilometres east of Tours on the north bank of the Loire. Take N152 to Vouvray, then D46 to Vernou sur Brenne. Follow signs for the Chateau de Jallanges.

CHATEAU DE JALLANGES
Host: Monsieur Stéphane Balin-Ferry
Vernou sur Brenne, 37210 Vouvray, France
tel: 47.52.01.71
3 Rooms, 2 Suites, all with pvt bath/WC
Double: 600-800F, Triple: 750-950F
Table d'Hôte: 200F per person
Open all year
Good English spoken
Region: Loire Valley

The attractive and friendly Porret family offer travellers comfortable accommodation in a newly renovated part of their chalet-style house. Monique and Joseph paid close attention to detail when remodelling their guest quarters, adding welcome conveniences such as a pine-panelled kitchen and completely independent entry. The four guest bedrooms are all very similar, each with a private shower and WC and French doors leading to a private balcony. A fresh, clean feeling pervades the rooms which are tastefully decorated with warm, textured wallcoverings and contemporary furniture. La Cascade is an ideal stopping place for travellers seeking reasonably priced, independent accommodation with modern comfort, located in the heart of the scenic French Alps. *Directions:* Vesonne is located approximately 30 kilometres south of Annecy via N508 in the direction of Albertville. About 3 kilometres before the town of Faverges, look for a sign for Col de la Forclaz (Forclaz Pass) to the left which leads through the village of Vesonne. Go through the village, following signs for Col de la Forclaz. Just after crossing a bridge, look for the Porrets' driveway on the left which is marked with a Chambres d'Hôtes sign.

LA CASCADE
Hosts: Monique and Joseph Porret
83 Chemin de la Forge
Vesonne, 74210 Faverges, France
tel: 50.44.65.48
4 Rooms, all with private shower/WC
Single: 130F, Double: 180F, Triple: 230F
No Table d'Hôte, but kitchen available
Open all year
Very little English spoken
Region: French Alps

Many of the chateaux that offer bed and breakfast are quite "homespun".   Not the Chateau de Veyrignac which is lots of fun and definitely a commercial operation. The English owner, Geoffrey Kenyon-May, is a man of many talents and boundless enthusiasm.   One of his many passions is restorations.   The Chateau de Veyrignac, dating back to feudal times, is one of his creative outlets.   The living areas are nicely decorated with many antiques, the bedrooms too have a few antiques - the more expensive are those with the best furnishings and superior views.   One of the very nicest aspects of the castle is its setting: a large terrace stretches out to a bluff which becomes a wooded drop off to the Dordogne river far below.   In another part of the garden is a lovely swimming pool.   Other fun features of the castle reflect hobbies of Geoffrey: a memorable collection of armor and old weapons, a "torture chamber" in the dungeons, a museum of life-sized figures intricately dressed in period costumes - even balloon rides are available. *Directions:* Sarlat is located 168 km east of Bordeaux.   From Sarlat go south on D704. Cross the bridge over the Dordogne and turn left at the first road which is the D50.   The way to Chateau Veyrignac well signposted.

CHATEAU DE VEYRIGNAC
Hosts: M & Mme Geoffrey Kenyon-May
Veyrignac
24370 Carlux, France
tel: 53.28.13.56 fax: 53.28.14.28
8 Rooms, all with private bath/WC
Double: 430-830F
No Table d'Hôte
Credit cards: All major
Open March to December
Fluent English spoken
Region: Périgord

Ginette and Yvon live in an idyllic mountain setting of which most city dwellers can only dream. Their friendly white furry dog and several tabby cats cluster at the threshold of their charming old chalet of regional stone and weathered wood. A very casual, home-like atmosphere reigns inside the 158-year-old house where Monsieur and Madame have raised five children and now offer guest accommodation in two attic bedrooms on the third floor. Rooms are furnished with wooden beds, tables and chairs and each has a private shower and washing area. Old exposed beams, rafters and natural wood walls add a rustic, mountain feeling, which is enhanced by the lovely view from the balconies over green meadows dotted with trees and wildflowers. The soothing sound of a rushing stream provides a restful nighttime lullabye. Chez Avrillon is a good base for hikers and travellers seeking simple comforts in an unspoilt Alpine setting. *Directions:* Les Villards sur Thones is located approximately 25 kilometres east of Annecy. Take D909 in the direction of La Clusaz which passes right by the town of Les Villards sur Thones. Just after town, turn to the right off the main road following a sign for Chambres d'Hôtes with a green arrow. Turn left at the next intersection and look for a driveway leading to the Avrillons' chalet on the right.

CHEZ AVRILLON
Hosts: Ginette and Yvon Avrillon
La Villaz, 74230 Les Villards sur Thones, France
tel: 50.02.04.30
2 Rooms with private showers, share 1 WC
Double: 150F, Triple: 210F
Table d'Hôte: 65F per person
Open all year
No English spoken
Region: French Alps

Villars les Dombes is a small town located in the heart of a forested region which is dotted with thousands of small lakes. The George family lives in a quiet suburb on the edge of town where they have been offering bed and breakfast accommodation to travellers for the last three years. Their house has thick stone walls and old beamed ceilings that attest to its 300-year-old history. The former attic has been renovated into a fresh, cheerful guest apartment offering a kitchenette, bedroom with private bath and a fold-out sofa in the sitting area. The bedroom is prettily decorated with blue flowered wallpaper and the bathroom is very modern, well-equipped and spotlessly clean. Exposed beams and a bouquet of daisies add charm to the kitchen and sitting area which is furnished in light pine furniture and pale green wallpaper. A stay with the Georges means a high level of comfort and privacy in a quiet setting. *Directions:* Villars les Dombes is located approximately 30 kilometres northeast of Lyon. Leaving Lyon, take N83, following signs for Strasbourg and Bourg en Bresse. Once in the town of Villars les Dombes, look for Chambres d'Hôtes signs across from the pharmacy. Follow directions on the signs, turning right and heading out of town for about a half mile, until another Chambres d'Hôtes sign directs into the George's driveway on the right.

CHEZ GEORGE
Hosts: Maurice and Therese George
Les Petits Communaux, 01130 Villars les Dombes, France
tel: 74.98.05.44
2 Rooms with private baths
Single: 152F, Double: 177F, Triple: 246F
No Table d'Hôte, kitchenette available to guests
Open all year
No English spoken
Region: South Burgundy

The Chateau de Villiers-le-Mahieu, whose origins date back to the 13th Century, will fulfill any childhood fantasy to live in a fairy-tale castle. The beautifully maintained castle is positioned in parklike grounds, manicured to perfection. Like a gem within this park, the chateau sits on its own little island surrounded by a moat. The main access is over a narrow bridge leading into the inner courtyard-garden, framed on three sides by the ivy covered stone walls of the chateau . The Chateau de Villiers-le-Mahieu is not a homey little castle where one becomes "chummy" with the owners, but rather a commercial operation with 18 guest rooms in the chateau and 11 in the garden annex. Splurge and request room "one", a grand room in the original castle, "wallpapered" in a handsome blue print fabric that repeats in the drapes the three tall French windows looking out to the gardens. In the park surrounding the castle there is a beautiful swimming pool and tennis courts. *Directions:* Located 40 km southwest of Paris. Take the A13 west from Paris. Exit south on A12 toward Dreux-Bois d/Arcy. Continue following the signs to Dreux until you come to Pontchartrain then take D11 signposted to Thoiry. As the road leaves Thoiry, turn left on D 45 toward Villiers le Mahieu and continue through the town and you will see signs to the chateau on the left side of the road.

CHATEAU DE VILLIERS-LE-MAHIEU
Host: M. Jean-Luc Chaufour
78770 Villiers-le-Mahieu, France
tel: 34.87.44.25 fax: 1.34.87.44.40
39 Rooms, all with private bath/WC
Double: 620-760F
Table d'Hôte: On request, 6 person minimum
Credit cards: AX, VS
Closed 1 week in August, 1 week at Christmas
Good English spoken
Region: Ile-de-France

Monsieur and Madame Portals' contemporary home is found on a scenic plateau high above Aix les Bains, with spectacular views over the surrounding granite peaks.   In this tranquil setting guests are two steps away from lovely walks on the wooded plateau, yet at the same time have the convenience of close-by civilization. Madame Portal is a very warm, cheerful hostess who makes sure her guests feel comfortable and at home.   Bedrooms are attractively furnished in a contemporary style and all open onto a balcony above the Portals' restful garden.   The house is built on a hillside, and there is a lower level where the Portals have installed a fully-equipped kitchen so that guests may prepare their own evening meals.   A flagstone terrace with a table and chairs opens out to the garden for a pleasant dinner setting. *Directions:* Viviers du Lac is located approximately 3 kilometres south of Aix les Bains.   Leave Aix following signs for Chambéry on N491 (do not take N201).   The road borders a golf course, and there will be a turnoff to the right marked Le Viviers du Lac.   Turn right towards Les Essarts at the central village square where there is a fountain, town hall and church.   Follow the curving road up a hill, veering right when the road forks.   At the top of the hill, look for the Portals' brown gate on the left.

CHEZ PORTAL
Hosts: Monsieur and Madame Portal
1193 Rte des Essarts, 73420 Le Viviers du Lac, France
tel: 79.61.44.61
3 Rooms, 1 with private bath,
 Other rooms share 1 bath/WC
Single: 187F, Double: 282F, Triple: 376F
No Table d'Hôte, kitchen available for guests
Open all year
No English spoken
Region: French Alps

James and Marie-Jose Hamel are a very friendly young couple who take great pleasure in welcoming guests to their manor home. Originally a fortress dating from the 12th century, Le Chateau was rebuilt in 1450 and again in 1750 and has a colourful history. The Hamels are fond of recounting the story of their most famous visitor, Andy Rooney of "60 Minutes" fame. He worked here as a journalist during World War II when the chateau was inhabited by the American Press Corps and recently revisited in 1984. Breakfast is served in the former press room complete with brass nameplate, in English, still intact on the door. A lofty ceiling, dark, pine-panelled walls and a lovely old tile floor provide intimate surroundings to begin the day or enjoy an evening aperitif. Guest bedrooms are tastefully furnished and decorated with handsome antiques and harmonious colour schemes. The rooms are found in a separate wing of the chateau, thus affording guests a convenient, private entry. *Directions:* Vouilly is located approximately 25 kilometres west of Bayeux. Take D5 west to Le Molay Littry, then turn right, continuing on D5 in the direction of Isigny sur Mer until you reach Vouilly. Just after entering Vouilly, look for a Chambres d'Hôtes sign directing you to turn right onto a winding road which you will follow to the Hamels' driveway.

LE CHATEAU
Hosts: James and Marie-Jose Hamel
Vouilly, 14230 Isigny sur Mer, France
tel: 31.22.08.59
3 Rooms, all w/ pvt bath, 1 w/ pvt WC
Single: 180F, Double: 230F, Triple: 280F
No Table d'Hôte, Ferme Auberge nearby
Open all year
Very little English spoken
Region: Normandy

Discoveries from Our Readers

Many of the places to stay newly featured in this edition are those you recommended to us and which we inspected and agreed wholeheartedly with your appraisal. However, there were some we never had the opportunity to see. We have a firm policy never to feature any Bed and Breakfast, no matter how perfect it sounds, until we have made a personal inspection. This seemed a waste of some excellent "tips", so, to solve this dilemma, the following section features places to stay that you have shared with us, but which we have not yet had the opportunity to visit. Thank you for your discoveries. Please keep them coming.

ARTANNES   CHATEAU DE LA MOTHE

REGION: LOIRE VALLEY Béatrice and Christian Lamy, Chateau de la Mothe, 9, rue de la Fontaine Sainte, 37260 Artannes, France; tel: 47.26.80.18, fax: 47.26.80.57; double 350F-450F; open April-September.

"The Chateau de la Mothe is a small chateau near Azay-le-Rideau, ideally located for touring the Loire area. Welcoming hosts Beatrice and Christian Lamy speak good English and are always happy to assist guests in planning their sightseeing. They offer one double room and two suites for four people, all with private bathrooms and WC. Our suite was very spacious, as was the bathroom, with lovely views out over the countryside. The guest sitting room has an old tile floor, bookcases and a large stone fireplace. Most of the rooms are accessed from the central tower's circular stone staircase and have lots of historic ambiance." *Recommended by Ambrose Wilson, Albuquerque, New Mexico.*

REGION: LOIRE VALLEY Jacqueline and Harry Courtot-Atterton, 36200 Bouesse, France; tel: 54.25.12.20, fax: 54.25.12.30; 5 bedrooms 430F to 530F, 6 apartments to 650F; breakfast 40F per person; closed in January.

We received a long, very enthusiastic letter about a hotel south of Paris in the Berry region that sounds lovely. "On a recent trip to France we encountered what we believe to be a real treasure located in a region that is overlooked by many travel writers - the Berry region in central France. Located just three hours from Paris, the Chateau de Bouesse offers an ideal stopping place for anyone journeying south along the N 20. It combines 15th-century adventure with modern comfort and elegant dining. The accommodations are beautiful and spacious. At present there are seven rooms, four that are in the grand style, and three, although smaller, still elegant. There are also several two-bedroom suites. All have new and modern bath facilities. Excellent as the food and accommodation are, it is the hosts that will make this stay memorable. Jacqueline and Harry Courtot-Atterton are Canadians who resettled in the Berry region about three years ago to restore "their chateau". It was a dream project for the two of them. Both are fluent in English, French and Spanish. As a result, guests are able to have a "typical French experience" within the protection of an English speaking environment. We came to the chateau for one night and ended up spending three nights. The restoration of the chateau has been a local project. Artisans are local people living within 15 kilometers of the chateau. There is pride and great personal identification with the project with the result that the completed work is superb in quality and detail. As much as we would like to keep this gem for ourselves, Jacqueline and Harry deserve a wider range of guests than just my wife and myself." *Recommended by Fran and Robert Smith, Berkeley, California*

CONTES DOMAINE LE CASTELLAR

REGION: CÔTE D'AZUR Francine Vélut, Domaine le Castellar, Route de Berre les Alpes, 06390 Contes, France; tel: 93.91.83.51; 2 bedrooms; approximate cost double 330F (be sure to put owner's name in mailing address).

About a 20-minute drive north of Nice along the Route de Berre Les Alpes, Madame Vélut offers two guest rooms in a pastel-pink stucco villa with the traditional light green shuttered windows and doors. One of the guest rooms is decorated in shades of blue, the other in pretty rose tones - both have modern, well-equipped bathrooms. The house opens onto a very pretty English garden. A guest wrote: "We had a marvelous experience and only wish we could stayed longer to enjoy the wonderful hospitality and the charming countryside, and the best breakfast in all of France". *Recommended by Angie and Marilyn.*

ENTRECHAUX L'ESCLERIADE

REGION: PROVENCE Marie-Jean and Vincent Gallo, L'Escleriade, Route de Saint-Marcellin, 84340 Entrechaux, France; tel: 90.46.01.32; 6 bedrooms, 4 with private bathroom; double 250F; open all year.

"We wish to highly recommend L'Escleriade run by Marie-Jean and Vincent Gallo. They have only been open a short while, but they are most charming hosts and the GITES is an absolute delight. It is a new building (built in the traditional style) in a most attractive setting. The bedrooms are prettily decorated. There are lovely views across the valley. We only intended to stay one night, but in fact stayed four nights, the atmosphere and friendliness of our hosts we found difficult to leave, as did other guests who stayed even longer than us." *Recommended by Marie and John Shannon, England.*

FONTEVRAUD L'ABBAYE   DOMAINE DE MESTRE

LOIRE VALLEY Dauge family, Le Domaine de Mestré, 49590 Fontevraud L'Abbaye, France; tel: 41.51.75.87; 12 rooms with private bathroom; double 340F; Table d'Hôte 120F; open all year.

"Domaine de Mestre is situated about 1.5 km outside of Fontevraud in the direction of the Loire river.   The inn is a former chateau used as a retreat by the monks who lived in the Abbaye de Fontevraud.   Today the chateau is home to the Dauge family, three generations of which operate the inn as well as a soap manufacturing enterprise called Martin de Candle.   Our room, almost a suite, was on the third (top) floor, in the corner, and was furnished with a queen bed, sitting chairs and writing table, and a large salle de bain.   The meals were served with pride by the senior Monsieur Dauge and were exceptional.   We stayed three nights and, needless to say, we left with some sorrow.   The inn requires reservations for its dining room.   The Dauge's make hand and laundry soap as well as bath oils, all incredible." *Recommended by Harry A. Oberhelman III, Santa Cruz, California.*

GRAMAT   MOULIN DE FRESQUET

REGION: PÉRIGORD Ramelot family, Moulin de Fresquet, 46500 Gramat, France; tel: 65.38.70.60; 5 rooms all with private bathroom; double from 230F to 260F; open all year; Table d'Hôte: 85F (including wine); a little English spoken.

We have a recommendation about a bed and breakfast that offers "comfortable guest rooms and family meals in the peace and quiet of an authentic water mill. All the rooms have private bathroom and are decorated in the spirit of the mill". Indeed the old stone mill looks most inviting with thick stone walls, beamed ceilings, appropriate country antiques and its own little stream which tunnels beneath a wing of the house.   We'd love more comments on this inn.

ISSIGEAC   LA CHARTREUSE DU SORD

REGION: PÉRIGORD Mme. Veronique Boddéle, La Chartreuse du Sord, Montaut 24560 Issigeac, France; tel: 53.58.76.70 fax: 53.58.15.94; 2 bedrooms; double 290F; open May through September.

"The Chartreuse is an old, one-story farm complex that is being restored by the charming couple that own and run it. The rooms have full-length door/windows that look out over the fields. They are spacious, clean and fresh, and comfortably appointed with contemporary furniture. The farm buildings date from Napoleon's time, and form a courtyard where one can enjoy breakfast in the morning sun. Madame Boddéle speaks some English and is hoping to learn more."
Recommended by Caryl Campbell and John Adams, Seattle, Washington

JOSSELIN   CHEZ GUYOT

REGION: BRITTANY, M and Mme Guyot, Butte Saint-Laurent, 56120 Josselin; tel: 97.22.22.09; 3 bedrooms, rate unknown.

"This note is a follow up on our recent conversation singing the praises of a Brittany B&B we found on a recent trip to France. The Guyots are located in a new hilltop house with 3 bedrooms available in Josselin, a small town ideally suited for an overnight stop going from St. Malo in Northern Brittany to Vannes in Southern Brittany (it is closer to Vannes). The Guyots do not speak English, but have a son (computer type) living in San Jose. They are natural hosts. Breakfast is rolls, baguetts, croissants, home made jam and local honey and Mme Goyot's crepes."
Recommended by Paul E. Boudakian, D.D.S., Berkeley, California.

MONTEILLE   FERME DES VERGÉES

REGION: NORMANDY Madame Claudine Guillaumin, Ferme des Vergées, Monteille 14270 Mézidon, France; tel: 31.63.01.13; 2 bedrooms, each with wash basin and toilet - share a bathroom; double 180F; open all year.

"Madame Claudine Guillaume speaks no English, but her daughter Christine, about 20, speaks English well. The house is a fascinating 300-year old Normandy farmhouse with barn in back, sheep in the meadow, apple orchard, corn, and cows. The surroundings are simply gorgeous. It is a short drive to the coast and all the towns and sights there, and a joy to return to. Madame Guillaume prepares a special breakfast in a wonderful old room where the fireplace is as large as most kitchens. Truly a slice of heaven." *Recommended by B.B., USA*

MONTRESOR   LA PENSION DE L'ABBAYE

REGION: LOIRE VALLEY Mme. Odile Rousseau, La Pension de L'Abbaye, rue de l'Abbaye, Villeloin-Coulange, 37460 Montresor, France; tel: 47.92.77.77, fax: 47.92.66.96; (winter months) 20 West 20th Street, apartment 903, New York, NY 10011; tel: 212-255-5961, fax: 212-989-5519; 3 rooms with private bathroom; double 275F; Table d'Hôte 100F; fluent English; open end of May to October.

"I discovered this pension last year. Not only were the rooms incredibly comfortable, but the atmosphere bespoke the beauty of this magical region with a 12th-century abbey's ramparts outside my window and the arches of the ruins of a Romanesque church in my room! Our hosts spoke fluent English. After a long day of touring, my wife and I would return to a delicious, several-course meal with robust local wines." Villeloin-Coulange is located about a 45-minute drive from Tours. *Recommended by Laban Hill, New York, New York.*

NICE	HOTEL DE LA MER

REGION: RIVIERA   Madame Feri Forouzan, Hotel de la Mer, 4, Place Massena, 06000 Nice, France; tel: 93.92.09.10   fax: 93.16.14.08; 12 rooms with private bathroom; double 350F to 400F; credit cards: all major; English spokent.

With a shortage of reasonably priced in Nice, we are glad to share with you the Hotel de la Mer, a two star pension well-located on the Place Messena.   "This past summer I spent a portion of my vacation in Nice and stayed at the Hotel de la Mer, which is a quaint hotel located directly on Place messena.   I would recommend this hotel to other travelers who are planning a trip to Nice.   Before I left, I spoke to Feri Forouzan to tell her how much I enjoyed my stay and that I would write to you upon my return." *Recommended by Brigitte Hoppe, Clifton, New Jersey*

ONZAIN	EN VAL DU LOIRE

REGION: LOIRE VALLEY   Martine Langlais, 46, rue de Meuves, 41150 Onzain, France; tel: 1.54.20.78.82   fax: 54.20.78.82; 5 rooms all with private bathroom; double 310F; open April to December.

"The first impression of this B&B is of its style and decor - truly French Country, with charm and class!   Each of the five rooms is beautifully appointed and the common areas are warm and inviting.   Yet it was the people that added the most important dimension to our wonderful stay.   Martine and George left Paris behind to make their B&B dream come true nine months ago, speak very good English and we were able to share in numerous interesting and animated conversations." *Recommended by P. & R. Tieman, USA.*

ROGER SUR BUCHY   LE CHATEAU

REGION: NORMANDY   Katia & Jacques Preterre-Rieux, Le Chateau, Place de l'Eglise, 76750 Bosc-Roger sur Buchy, France; tel: 35.34.29.70; 4 rooms; double 300F; open March to January; English spoken; no restaurant.

"We so enjoyed our stay at Le Chateau that we'd like others to as well. Le Chateau is a large attractive house set on large grounds in a small, friendly village. Katia and her husband are cosmopolitan, warm hosts, friendly yet not intrusive, and speak good English.   Our room was large and comfortable, with thoughtful extras such as magazines and little candies provided." *Recommended by Chuck and Kaye Cook-Kollars, Beverly, Massachusetts.*

SACHÉ   MANOIR DE BECHERON

REGION: LOIRE VALLEY   Madame Jacquet, Manoir de Becheron, Saché, 37190 Azay-le-Rideau, France; tel: 47.26.86.26; approximate cost double 350F.

"The manoir is a grand house with a history. Restored beautifully by Martine Jacquet and her husband, the house dates from the 17th Century (although the pigeon tower is from the 14th Century). More recently it was owned by Jo Davidson, American sculptor and father-in-law of Alexander Calder. Madame Jacquet has three rooms to let, all with full bathroom accommodations. Ours, the largest of the three, had a huge bedroom, a study in the pigeon tower and a large bathroom almost the size of the bedroom. A delicious continental breakfast was served in the stately dining room. Madame Jacquet, who speaks some English, was most hospitable and was pleased to suggest routes for us to explore in the area." *Recommended by anonymous readers from Albany, New York.*

SAINT-LÈONS   CHATEAU DE SAINT-LEONS

REGION: GORGES DU TARN: Odile & Marc Chodkiewicz, Chateau de Saint-Lèons, 12780 Saint-Lèons, France; tel: 33.65.61.84.85   fax: 33.65.61.82.30; 3 rooms (2 with private bathroom, 1 with washbasin in room); double 320F; Table d'Hôte 100F; open all year; fluent English spoken.

Chateau de Saint-Lèons looks just fabulous: a wonderful 15th-century turreted castle in the small village of Saint-Lèons in southern France. Marc Chodkiewicz loves to cook and most of the food served is freshly picked from the garden (he is even writing a cookbook). Odile is an artist - specializing in watercolors - many of her paintings adorn the walls of the chateau. We would love more feedback from travellers on this picture-book perfect little castle.

ST PHILBERT-DES-CHAMPS   LA FERME DES POIRIERS ROSES

REGION: NORMANDY. M and Mme Jacques Lecorneur, La Ferme des Poiriers Roses, Saint Philbert des Champs, 14130 Pont L'eveque, France; tel: 31.64.72.14; 5 rooms; approximate cost double 480F; open from March to mid-November.

We are delighted to share with you a wonderful looking, timbered farmhouse in the countryside near Lisieux. We received a large packet of information along with the with colored photographs showing such an interior with hand-hewn beamed ceilings, walls decorated with copper pots and dried bouquets of colorful flowers, many country antiques, and casement windows overlooking trees and meadows. This truly looks like a winner and we will certainly include this old farmhouse B&B on our next research trip and in the meantime will hope to hear from more readers.

SAVONNIÈRES   PRIEURÉ DES GRANGES

REGION: LOIRE VALLEY   Philippe Dufresne, Prieuré des Granges, Route de Ballan, 37510 Savonnières, France; tel: 47.50.09.67; approximate cost double 400F.

The Prieuré des Granges dates from the 17th and 19th Centuries and is located in a several acres of parklike grounds.   The large rooms face south, have private baths, and are furnished with many antique pieces.   The owner, Philippe Dufresne, speaks fluent English and, along with co-host, Serge Carre, enjoys welcoming Americans to their bed and breakfast.   There are several restaurants in nearby Savonnières, and "Table d'Hôte" dinners are also available with advance notice at the Prieuré des Granges. *Recommended an anonymous reader from Manhattan Beach, CA*

VERSAILLES   LA RESIDENCE DU BERRY

REGION: PARIS.   Pierre Lansard and son, Manuel, La Residence du Berry, 14 Rue d'Anjou, 78000 Versailles, France; tel: 1.39.49.07.07, fax: 1.30.50.59.40; 38 rooms; approximate cost double 360F to 420F.

"The Lansard Family that runs the Hotel Du Berry was the most friendly of all the places we visited on our last trip to France.   The father let me check out many of the rooms until I found the *perfect one*, a large room on the upper floor with a beam ceiling.   They were very helpful recommending places that were cooperative for car service, laundry, banking and dining.   They made our stay in Versailles memorable.   We made a great side trip to Fontainebleau and Vaux Le Viconte (the latter gardens should not be missed).   We also did Paris from there by train which avoided the brutal Paris traffic on weekdays." *Recommended by Dr and Mrs Weeks, Oakland, California.*

INDEX

INDEX

INDEX

INDEX

INDEX

INDEX

INDEX

INDEX

DISCOVERIES FROM OUR READERS

"Discoveries from Our Readers" features places to stay that sound excellent, but which we have not yet had an opportunity to visit. If you have a favorite hideaway that you would be willing to share with other readers, we would love to hear from you. The type of accommodations we feature are those with old world ambiance, special charm, and warmth of welcome. Please send the following information:

1. *Your name, address and telephone number.*

2. *Name, address and telephone number of your discovery.*

3. *Rate for a double room including tax, service and breakfast.*

4. *Brochure or picture (we cannot return material).*

5. *Permission to use an edited version of your description.*

6. *Would you want your name, city, and state included in the book?*

Please send to:

Karen Brown's Country Inn Guides, Post Office Box 70, San Mateo, CA 94401, USA
Telephone (415) 342-5591   Fax (415) 342-9153

Karen Brown's Country Inn Guides

The Most Reliable Series on Charming Places to Stay

KAREN BROWN'S
FRENCH
Country Inns & Itineraries

UPDATED AND REVISED • SIXTH EDITION

KAREN BROWN'S
CALIFORNIA
Country Inns & Itineraries

UPDATED AND REVISED • SECOND EDITION

KAREN BROWN'S
ITALIAN
Country Inns & Itineraries

UPDATED AND REVISED • FOURTH EDITION

KAREN BROWN'S
FRENCH
Country Bed & Breakfasts

UPDATED AND REVISED • SECOND EDITION

KAREN BROWN'S
ENGLISH
Country Bed & Breakfasts

UPDATED AND REVISED • SECOND EDITION

KAREN BROWN'S
GERMAN
Country Inns & Itineraries

UPDATED AND REVISED • THIRD EDITION

KAREN BROWN'S
ITALIAN
Country Bed & Breakfasts

NEW • FIRST EDITION

KAREN BROWN'S
ENGLISH, WELSH & SCOTTISH
Country Hotels & Itineraries

UPDATED AND REVISED • SIXTH EDITION

Order Form

KAREN BROWN'S COUNTRY INN GUIDES

Please ask in your local bookstore for KAREN BROWN'S COUNTRY INN guides.
If the books you want are unavailable, you may order directly from the publisher.

_____ *Austrian Country Inns & Castles (1988 edition) $6.00*
_____ *California Country Inns & Itineraries $14.95*
_____ *English Country Bed & Breakfasts $13.95*
_____ *English, Welsh & Scottish Country Hotels & Itineraries $14.95*
_____ *French Country Bed & Breakfasts $13.95*
_____ *French Country Inns & Itineraries $14.95*
_____ *German Country Inns & Itineraries $14.95*
_____ *Irish Country Inns (1988 edition) $6.00*
_____ *Italian Country Bed & Breakfasts $13.95*
_____ *Italian Country Inns & Itineraries $14.95*
_____ *Portuguese Country Inns & Pousadas $12.95*
_____ *Scandinavian Country Inns & Manors (1987 edition) $6.00*
_____ *Spanish Country Inns & Paradors $12.95*
_____ *Swiss Country Inns & Chalets (1989 edition) $6.00*

Name _____ Street _____

City _____ State _____ Zip _____ tel: _____

Credit Card (Mastercard or Visa) _____ Exp: _____

Add $3.50 for the first book and .50 for each additional book for postage & packing.
California residents add 8.25% sales tax.
Indicate number of copies of each title; send form with check or credit card information to:

KAREN BROWN'S COUNTRY INN GUIDES
Post Office Box 70, San Mateo, California, 94401, U.S.A.
Tel: (415) 342-9117   Fax: (415) 342-9153

Karen Brown's
French Country Inns & Itineraries

The Choice of the Discriminating Traveller to France

Featuring Charming Small Hotels and Inns
And Detailed Itineraries for Exploring the Countryside

French Country Inns & Itineraries is the perfect companion guide to Karen Brown's *French Country Bed & Breakfasts*. Whereas the Bed & Breakfast guide has "hand-picked" the choice places to stay in private homes, the *French Country Inns & Itineraries* book features accommodations with great charm in small hotels and inns. All the pertinent information is given: description of the accommodation, sketch, price, driving directions, maps, if there is a restaurant, owner's name, telephone and fax number, dates open, etc.

KAREN BROWN'S
FRENCH
Country Inns & Itineraries

UPDATED AND REVISED • SIXTH EDITION

French Country Inns & Itineraries does not replace *French Country Bed & Breakfasts* - together they make the perfect pair for the traveller who wants to explore the countryside of France. Both feature places to stay with charm, warmth of welcome and old world ambiance: *French Country Bed & Breakfasts* features places to stay in private homes; *French Country Inns & Itineraries* features small hotels and inns PLUS the added bonus of 11 itineraries, handy for use with the bed & breakfast guide. Each book uses the same maps so it is easy to choose a combination of places to stay from each, adding great variety for where to spend the night.

KAREN BROWN wrote her first travel guide, *French Country Inns & Chateaux*, in 1979. This original guide is now in its 6th edition plus 13 books have been added to the series which has become known as the most personalized, reliable reference library for the discriminating traveller. Although Karen's staff has expanded, she is still involved in the publication of her guide books. Karen, her husband, Rick, their daughter, Alexandra, and son, Richard, live on the coast south of San Francisco at their own country inn, Seal Cove Inn, in Moss Beach, California.

KIRSTEN PRICE, author of *French Country Bed & Breakfasts*, was born and raised in the San Francisco Bay area where she has been a friend of Karen's since grade-school days. Kirsten, who has a gift for foreign languages, has divided her time for the past 10 years between Colorado, New Zealand and Europe - teaching skiing, leading bike tours to France, working in the resort/travel industry and researching for the Karen Brown guides. Kirsten now lives in San Francisco.

CLARE BROWN, CTC, has many years of experience in the field of travel and has earned the designation of Certified Travel Consultant. Since 1969 she has specialized in planning itineraries to Europe using charming small hotels in the countryside for her clients. The focus of her job remains unchanged, but now her expertise is available to a larger audience - the readers of her daughter's Country Inn guides. Clare lives in the San Francisco Bay area with her husband, Bill.

BARBARA TAPP, the talented artist responsible for all of the hotel sketches and delightful illustrations in this guide, was raised in Australia where she studied in Sydney at the School of Interior Design. Although Barbara continues with freelance projects, she devotes much of her time to illustrating Karen's Country Inn guides. Barbara lives in the San Francisco Bay area with her husband, Richard, their two sons, Jonothan and Alexander, and young daughter, Georgia.

JANN POLLARD, the artist responsible for the beautiful painting on the cover of this guide, has studied art since childhood, and is well-known for her outstanding impressionistic-style water colors which she has exhibited in numerous juried shows, winning many awards. Jann travels frequently to Europe (using Karen Brown's guides) where she loves to paint old world architecture. Jann lives in the San Francisco Bay area with her husband, Gene, and two daughters.

SEAL COVE INN - LOCATED IN THE SAN FRANCISCO AREA

Karen (Brown) Herbert is best known as a writer and publisher of the Karen Brown's Country Inn guides, favorites of travellers searching for the most charming country inns throughout Europe and California. Now Karen and her husband, Rick, have put sixteen years of experience into reality and opened their own superb hideaway, Seal Cove Inn. Spectacularly set amongst wildflowers and bordered by towering cypress trees, Seal Cove Inn looks out to the ocean over acres of county park: an oasis where you can enjoy secluded beaches, explore tide-pools, watch frolicking seals, and follow the tree-lined path tracing the windswept ocean bluffs. Country antiques, lovely original watercolors, flower-filled cradles, rich fabrics, and the gentle ticking of grandfather clocks create the perfect ambiance for a foggy day in front of the crackling log fire. Each bedroom is its own private haven with a comfortable sitting area before a wood-burning fireplace and doors opening onto a private patio with views to the distant ocean. Moss beach is a 30-minute drive south of San Francisco, 6 miles north of the picturesque town of Half Moon Bay, and a few minutes from Princeton harbor with its colorful fishing boats and restaurants. Seal Cove Inn makes a perfect base for whale-watching expeditions, salmon-fishing excursions, day trips to San Francisco, exploring the coast, or, best of all, just a romantic interlude by the sea - time to relax and be pampered. Karen and Rick are looking forward to meeting and welcoming you to their own inn.

Seal Cove Inn, 221 Cypress Avenue, Moss Beach, California, 94038, U.S.A.
telephone: (415) 728-7325   fax: (415) 728-4116